Translation of

Computer Languages

HOLDEN-DAY COMPUTER AND INFORMATION SCIENCES SERIES

S. D. Conte, Editor

Translation of
Computer Languages

Frederick W. Weingarten
National Science Foundation

Holden-Day, Inc.
San Francisco
Düsseldorf
Johannesburg   London
Panama   Singapore
Sydney   Toronto

To Dona

Cover photograph by Betty Berenson

TRANSLATION OF COMPUTER LANGUAGES

Library of Congress Catalog Card Number: 72-83240
ISBN: 0-8162-9423-2

Printed in the United States of America

1 2 3 4 5 6 7 8 9 0   MP   8 0 7 9 8 7 6 5 4 3

preface

In its early days, computer science was thought by many to be concerned primarily with the design of large electronic calculators and the development of programs for them. It all sounded pretty technological to scholars, and frustrated computer scientists trying to argue for their discipline as a science grew tired of only having algebraic automata theory to refer to as a scientifically rigorous study. As the years have passed, we have discovered concepts and approaches—such as information, algorithm, and computer language—that seem unique to computer science and that provide a basic underpinning to the discipline. These topics constantly come up, incorporating an algorithmic approach, in most of the currently important areas of study in computer science, indicative of an intellectual maturing of the discipline.

Another characteristic of a natural science is the existence of a continuum between those who study it theoretically and those who try and apply the knowledge, for example, the connection between theoretical biochemists and those seeking a cure for cancer. Or, consider as another example the bridge between theoretical physics and those scientists and engineers developing new sources of energy. It matters less how far the bridge stretches from the theoretical to the applied, then that it exists. For some time, the bridge did not exist in computer science, or at least its form, if there, was only barely visible.

Now such a continuum is developing, for example, between those people developing operating systems or designing machines and those theoreticians studying properties of information systems.

One example of the growth of such a bridge was the field of computer languages. Early compilers were written with no theoretical understanding of the properties of languages, and we are still suffering from the effects of language design carried on with no consideration of the basic properties of languages. Then, as we developed a discipline of language theory, spurred by the development of ALGOL 60, the whole approach to compiler writing and language design became increasingly rigorous. Out of this theoretical work came enormous practical benefits in terms of improved efficiency of compilers and usefulness of the languages to the programmer. In this case, between theory and practice, the bridge is fully developed.

This book is about this particular bridge. It is a discussion of the body of algorithmic theory behind the translation of computer (and, in fact, natural) languages. As such it can stand alone as a text for undergraduate course A-1 suggested by the Committee of Curriculum in Computer Science of the Association for Computing Machinery. The text has deliberately been kept small rather than encyclopedic, however, so that it can be used as a text for part of a course in either compiler writing or natural-language translation.

Its approach is algorithmic rather than mathematical, and thus it is not appropriate for a course in context-free languages. Instead, it presents those elements of the theory useful to students of computer software and system design. For the student who eventually will study automata and language theory, it provides an intuitive introduction and motivation for the work to follow. Mathematical notation is used, especially in Chapters 1, 3, 4, and 5, but the student with little mathematical background should be able to cope with the material.

I hope that this book will help span the gap developing between teaching the theoretical and applied aspects of translation. One has only to look at the typical pair of courses on computer language taught to computer-science students to see what I mean. In one course, formal grammars and their finite automaton translators are discussed as a branch of semigroup theory. Thus the course is an advanced mathematics course too difficult for students with little mathematical background. In the other course, the staff system programmer talks about writing compilers in terms of the tricks he has learned over the years. Thus much detail important to the compiler, but not significant to the structure, disappears. As a result, the course lacks rigor and reference to the body of important theoretical work in this field. Unfortunately, one common tendency of science is showing up here, the tendency to compartmentalize, to separate and move different areas of study further apart in efforts to become "pure," on the one hand, and "avoid the ivory tower," on the other hand. Now, in fact, we hear some voices speaking for two departments, one for pure computer science and one for software engineering. Separate but equal facilities and budgets are proposed, of course. This compartmentalization defeats the bridging process I consider vital to the maturing of a discipline.

As a final but most important note, I would like to thank the people who helped me assemble and prepare this weighty tome. Thanks to Debbie Voss, Sue Surrell, and Mary Childs for their efforts in typing it, and to the poor suffering students who had to work their way through initial drafts. Thanks, too, to Walter Stutzman for helping in proofing the final copy and in checking out the problems and algorithms. And thanks to my wife Dona, for her patient support and ready encouragement when it was most needed.

Frederick W. Weingarten

contents

1

preliminary concepts

Since the earliest days of computing, people trying to use computers have chafed against having to communicate with them in the computer's own language. To a computer, instructions and data are simply patterns of binary bits stored in its memory. Even when a programmer uses the symbol *5* to represent the pattern of bits *101*, he is coding the hardware language into a form more convenient to him. The use of *octal* (three binary bits) or *hexadecimal* (four binary bits) representation was the first small step toward making communication with the computer more natural. Since then, there has been a steady evolution toward the complex and sophisticated languages of today.

There are three major functions motivating and influencing this development of programming languages. They are the *mnemonic*, the *paradigm* (or *stereotype*), and the *data-control* functions. The most common general purpose languages show characteristics motivated by all of these factors, but there are many special purpose languages that stress primarily one particular function.

The mnemonic capability is the ability to substitute symbols and phrases that make sense to a human being for machine-language constructs. For example, most (but not all!) computing languages have a **Go to** command whose function is to transfer program control to another location in the code. This command corresponds directly with a single machine command expressed as a sequence of bits or numerical symbols. The argument of the **Go to** command is also a mnemonic construction. The programmer has, at some time, given a name to a location in his program. He can refer to that name throughout the program without worrying where it will be physically in memory.

The paradigm function is the ability to accumulate several minor instruction steps into larger, more logically complete groups that make more sense to the programmer. Coding input and output routines is a complex task, for example, which is done for the programmer in higher-level languages. When he uses a **Print** or **Read** statement, he is calling up large chunks of machine-language code that control the devices and his data. Another example is the scientist who when trying to solve an algebraic equation wishes to write it in its mathematical form—and let that form stand for the lengthy sequence of fetches, arithmetic operations, and stores at the machine level. Subroutines, functions, and a variety of macro facilities allow the programmer to construct even more complex stereotypes.

This paradigm facility of higher-level languages allows an increase in the complexity of systems that can be constructed. For an analogy, look at tennis. Each stroke in tennis has several points for the student to learn: foot position, backswing, forward stroke, and follow-through. And each of these points may have many smaller elements the player must remember. Until the beginning player masters these strokes so that he can call on them without consciously thinking about every step, he cannot put them together in a game. When learned, these strokes become basic elements he can put together in complex sequences. Later he may develop combinations of strokes and strategies that will become the basic elements of his game. In a similar way, a very large program is written by developing increasingly complex instruction stereotypes that become the basic elements of the program.

The final factor influencing programming language is data structure. The basic data structure in most computers is a linear array of units composed of some fixed number of bits. On some machines the units are character size, eight bits long, and are called *bytes*. On other computers the units are called *words* and range in size from 12 to 60 bits in length, depending on the machine. These units of storage are further characterized by having absolute addresses; that is, each unit has a single unique name designated for it. However, this type of storage structure is extremely restrictive for dealing with the wide variety of data types used by computer programmers. Thus there is the *logical data structure*, that structure used by the programmer in developing his algorithm, and the *physical data structure*, the representation of the data in the hardware itself. Many languages have been written to allow the programmer to state his algorithms in terms of the logical structure of his data rather than requiring him to write the physical-structure equivalent of the algorithm. The most common example in elementary programming is the *array*. By declaring, for instance, by the **Dimension** statement in FORTRAN, that a variable *MAT* is a two-dimensional array, the programmer can refer to an element *MAT*(*I, J*) in the array without bothering to calculate the physical location of the element within the matrix storage area.

There is a fourth motivation for higher-order computer languages that is not so directly apparent in their design. That motivation is the desire for *machine independence*. That is, one would like to write programs that are independent of any specific computer. Higher-order languages, in theory at least, allow that facility. While complete independence is rarely, if ever, achieved in practice, programs written in FORTRAN, COBOL, BASIC, and so on can be run on other computers with relatively small programming effort for modification compared to the work involved in writing them in the first place.

1.1 translation

Now that the programmer has been offered the convenience of the devices of a higher-order language, it is left to the computer to read the program written in it and deduce what sequence of machine instructions was intended. This process is generally called *compilation*. The *compiler* is a program in the computer that reads the program written, for example, in FORTRAN and generates a machine-language program that does whatever the FORTRAN instructions specify.

This compilation process consists of two main parts: the *translation* of the source language and the *generation* of machine-level code. The translation process unravels the statements of the source code into an intermediate representation containing enough information for the generation stage to proceed with the program construction. In English courses, sentences are sometimes taken apart, or *parsed*, and put in a diagram form that shows explicitly the relationships of the words and the role they play in the sentence. This process is independent of the specific meaning of the sentence, although it occasionally allows the student to understand a vague statement. In this book, parsing and translating will be used synonymously, for translation in compilation is a process quite analogous to the parsing of English sentences. The book will further be concerned with the theory and techniques behind the translation process.

The end result of the algorithms will be a form of diagram explicitly showing the relationship between parts of the source program, and serving as an intermediate representation of the program. The compiler then uses this representation either to directly generate the program code, or to operate directly from it in an *interpretive* mode. When interpreting, the processor does not produce a program for later execution, but rather directly performs the machine operations called for as it reads the intermediate form. Some very well known time-sharing language processors are interpretive in this manner, among them most BASIC and APL compilers. Interpretive processors allow for very fast compilation but, in general, suffer from slower execution. The decision of which mode to use, then, depends on the anticipated use of the compiler.

1.2   data structures

Before proceeding to the discussion of translation algorithms, it is necessary to review a few concepts from programming and mathematics. The book assumes that the student has studied programming and elementary data structures, so the review is merely to establish a standard nomenclature and refresh a few concepts. If these concepts seem new or confusing, a review of one of the many books on basic computer science might be in order.

The most commonly used data structure in translator writing is the *push-down stack*, also referred to as *last-in—first-out* (LIFO) storage. The stack is a linear sequence of storage location with a variable but bounded length. There are two addresses that refer to the stack, the *Base* and the *Head*, and all references to the contents of the stack must be made with reference to one or the other. The stack is built from the *Base;* that is, the Ith element in the stack is in the location $Base + I - 1$. Items are always both added to and deleted from the top of the stack, called the *Head*. Schematically a stack is represented as follows:

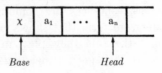

There are various ways of checking that the stack is empty. In this book an empty stack will be represented by a special character stored at the bottom. The symbol χ in the preceding figure indicates the bottom of the stack.

Adding a symbol z to a stack is referred to as *pushing* z on the stack. The contents of *Head* are incremented by one, and z is stored in the location pointed to by the new value of *Head*. After pushing z on the stack above, it looks as follows:

Deleting a symbol from a stack is called *popping* the stack. In this case, the value of *Head* is decremented by one. The results of popping a stack are the contents of the deleted cell. Thus the command to pop a stack may have an additional part designating a destination for the deleted contents, as in **Pop** *Stack* **to** *Temp*. If no argument is given, the contents are presumed deleted. Two pop operations on the above stack result in the following configuration.

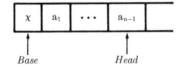

When writing a translator or, for that matter, any algorithm that manipulates symbolic data, it is common to use *lists*. They will not be referred to explicitly in the algorithms developed in this book, but implementation of these algorithms could involve list techniques ranging from elementary to quite sophisticated. The reader, as he programs the translations described in this book, should use list procedures to the extent that they help his project; but remember that no algorithm requires them.

List processing itself is a topic large enough for several books. An intuitive definition is that a list consists of *elements*, where each element, or *node*, contains two types of information: *intrinsic* information characterizing the node and *explicit* information about the relation between that node and others in the list. This explicit relational information is stored as *pointers*, addresses of other nodes in the list. The simplest list is the *string*, which is used to store a sequence of symbols $a_1, a_2, \ldots, a_n$. Each node contains a symbol, for example,

a_i, and a pointer to the node containing the next symbol a_{i+1}. Schematically, the list appears as follows:

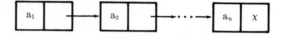

This time the symbol χ is used to designate the end of the string.

More complex list structures than the above can be built up, since, in theory, as many pointers as necessary can be added to any node. However, some of the better-known list-processing languages are based on a dual address scheme, where each node contains at most two addresses. Actually, both systems can be shown to be equivalent.

1.3   mathematical concepts—sets

The mathematics in this book will be primarily used for its notational and descriptive capacity rather than for the purpose of developing a rigorous mathematical theory. There will be some theorems, especially in Chapters 3, 4, and 5, but the mathematics is not essential to understanding the algorithms at an intuitive level. This orientation should not suggest that mathematics is not useful in this field. The theory of context-free languages has been developed in terms of some very sophisticated mathematics including the algebraic theory of semigroups and category theory. However, this book will be using only elementary and highly intuitive mathematical concepts that most readers have likely met on occasion. For completeness, let us review them here.

Definition 1.1:   A *set* is an unordered collection of objects called *elements*. The elements can be anything that can be named or defined by a rule.

Two ways of designating a set are by listing the names of the elements, or by specifying a rule that can test any object for membership in the set. Such a rule is called a *predicate* and is a function of all objects such that, if p is a predicate and x an object, then either

$$p(\text{x}) = \textbf{True}$$

if x is in the set, or

$$p(\text{x}) = \textbf{False}$$

if it is not.

Sets will be designated by capital Greek letters.   For example, let Σ be a set.   It can then be defined either as a collection of elements

$$\Sigma = \{a_1, a_2, \ldots, a_n\}$$

or as a predicate

$$\Sigma = \{x \mid p(x)\}$$

That is, x is an element of Σ if and only if $p(x) = \textbf{True}$.   The fact that an object x is an element of a set Σ is designated by the notation

$$x \in \Sigma$$

There is a special set appropriately referred to as the *empty set* or *null set* designated here by $\varnothing$.   This set contains no elements, but it is considered to exist anyway for the completeness of the theory.

There are three common binary set operations, defined as follows.

Definition 1.2:   The *union* of two sets Σ and T, written

$$\Sigma \cup T$$

is

$$\Sigma \cup T = \{x \mid x \in \Sigma \textbf{ or } x \in T\}$$

Definition 1.3:   The *intersection* of two sets Σ and T, written

$$\Sigma \cap T$$

is

$$\Sigma \cap T = \{x \mid x \in \Sigma \textbf{ and } x \in T\}$$

Definition 1.4:   The *difference* of two sets Σ and T, written

$$\Sigma - T$$

is

$$\Sigma - T = \{x \mid x \in \Sigma \textbf{ and } x \notin T\}$$

Usually, when working with sets, the elements are related in some sense; that is, they share some universal characteristics.   For example, they may be all numbers, all integers, all points in a plane, or all English words.   In other words, there is a *universal set* $\mathfrak{U}$, which contains all of the objects under consideration.   There is also a unary set operation that uses the universal set.

Definition 1.5:   The *complement* of a set Σ, written $\bar{\Sigma}$, is

$$\bar{\Sigma} = \mathfrak{U} - \Sigma$$

The complement of Σ is the set of all elements in the universe that are not in Σ.

There are some common relationships among sets that will be used later. We will, however, state them here.

Definition 1.6:   Two sets Σ and T are *equal*

$$\Sigma = T$$

when

x $\in \Sigma$ if and only if x $\in$ T

That is, the two sets are equal if and only if they contain exactly the same elements.

Definition 1.7:   A set Σ is a *subset* of a set T

$$\Sigma \subseteq T$$

if and only if all elements in Σ are also in T; that is, x $\in \Sigma$ implies that x $\in$ T. A set Σ is a *proper subset* of T, $\Sigma \subset$ T, if $\Sigma \subseteq$ T but $\Sigma \neq$ T.

1.4 *strings*

Sentences and program statements are composed of sequences of symbols, and in developing a theory of languages and their translators such sequences, called strings, must be dealt with.

Definition 1.8:   A *string* is an ordered sequence of elements

$$(a_1, a_2, \ldots , a_n)$$

When no confusion is possible, the parentheses and commas can be ignored, and the string written more compactly as

$$a_1 a_2 \cdots a_n$$

Strings can be designated by a single symbol, in which case a bar is put over the symbol. Thus $\bar{x}$ represents a string, while x represents a single element.

Strings are constructed from elements or other strings by a *concatenation* operator, represented by a centered dot. If

$$\bar{a} = a_1 a_2 \cdots a_n$$

and

$$\bar{b} = b_1 b_2 \cdots b_m$$

then

$$\bar{a} \cdot \bar{b} = a_1 a_2 \cdots a_n b_1 b_2 \cdots b_m$$

Again, when no confusion can result, the operator can be ignored, and the concatenation written $\bar{a}\bar{b}$.

As in sets, there is a special string that can be introduced, the *null string*, designated by ε. The concatenation operator is defined to operate with the null string in the following way. Let $\bar{a}$ be a string. Then

$$\bar{a} \cdot \varepsilon = \varepsilon \cdot \bar{a} = \bar{a}$$

Definition 1.9: A substring of a string $\bar{a}$ is a contiguous piece of $\bar{a}$. That is, if

$$\bar{a} = a_1 a_2 \cdots a_n$$

then

$$\bar{b} = b_1 b_2 \cdots b_m$$

is a substring of $\bar{a}$ if and only if there is an index $i \geq 1$ such that

$$b_1 = a_i$$
$$b_2 = a_{i+1}$$
$$\cdot$$
$$\cdot$$
$$\cdot$$
$$b_m = a_{i+m-1} \qquad \text{where } i + m - 1 \leq n$$

The concatenation operator can be carried over to sets as follows.

Definition 1.10: The *concatenation* of two sets, $\Sigma \cdot T$, is the set

$$\{\bar{a}\bar{b} \mid \bar{a} \in \Sigma \textbf{ and } \bar{b} \in T\}$$

If, for example,

$$\Sigma = \{a, b\} \qquad \text{and} \qquad T = \{c, d\}$$

then

$$\Sigma \cdot T = \{ac, ad, bc, bd\}$$

and

$$\Sigma \cdot \Sigma = \{aa, ab, ba, bb\}$$

The latter form can, for convenience, be written Σ^2. In general, extending the notation, Σ^n is the set of all strings of length m composed of elements of Σ. The length of a string $\bar{a}$ is indicated by the notation $|\bar{a}|$ so, if $\bar{a} \in \Sigma^n$, then $|\bar{a}| = n$.

Also, given any finite set Σ, there is a special set, Σ^*, constructed from it.

Definition 1.11: The *free semigroup* of a set Σ is the set

$$\Sigma^* = \{\bar{a} \mid \bar{a} \in \Sigma^n \text{ for some n } \textbf{or } \bar{a} = \varepsilon\}$$

That is, for each $\bar{a}$ in Σ^*, either $\bar{a}$ is the null string or there is some n such that $\bar{a} \in \Sigma^n$. Thus $\bar{a}$ is a finite string; $|\bar{a}| = n$; and the elements of ā are all in Σ. Since n can be arbitrarily large, Σ* is an infinite set, but all elements of Σ* are finite strings.

1.5 graphs

Another concept needed when discussing a mathematical theory of language derives from a more general mathematical construct than strings. This is the concept of a graph.

Definition 1.12: A *graph* is a set Σ of elements called *nodes*, and a set Φ of node pairs {a, b} called *branches*.

Intuitively, the nodes can be viewed as points arbitrarily distributed in space and the sets of node pairs can be considered instructions on connecting them. Thus the graph

$$\Sigma = \{a, b, c, d\}$$
$$\Phi = \{\{a, b\}, \{b, c\}, \{c, d\}, \{d, a\}\}$$

describes either of the two intuitive diagrams in Figure 1.1.

Definition 1.13: A *directed graph* is a graph for which the branches are ordered pairs called *directed branches*.

That is, the directed branch is oriented in the sense that directed branch (a, b) is different from (b, a). This difference is expressed graphically by an arrow pointing from the left-hand node, called the *tail*, to the right-hand node, called the *head*, and notationally by use of parentheses instead of brackets to designate a branch. Two directed graphs are shown in Figure 1.2.

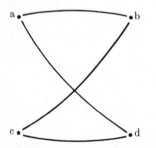
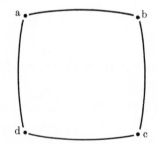

Figure 1.1 Two forms of graph with nodes {a, b, c, d}

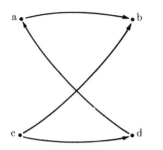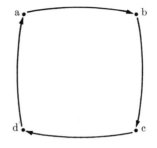

Figure 1.2   Two forms of a directed graph with nodes {a, b, c, d}

Definition 1.14:   A *path* is a sequence of nodes a_1, a_2, . . . , a_m, ($m \geq 2$) such that there is a branch between a_i and a_{i+1} for all $1 \leq i \leq m - 1$.

In terms of directed graphs, a path is a sequence of branches for which the head of one branch is the tail of the next. Thus in Figure 1.2, there is a path from d to a.

Definition 1.15:   Two nodes are said to be *connected* if and only if there is a path from one to the other.

In Figure 1.2 a and c are connected, as are d and b.

1.6   trees

The graph structure used most often in language theory and used here is the *tree*. Although trees can be defined in many ways, we will use the following definition.

Definition 1.16:   A tree is a directed graph in which

(a)   All nodes but one (the *root*) are at the head of only one branch.
(b)   The root is not at the head of any branch.
(c)   The root is connected with every node in the tree.

Figure 1.3 provides a schematic representation of a tree. Node a is its root. Arrows are not necessary once the root is known, since the directions of the branches can be traced out from it. To indicate the directions, the graph is generally oriented, depending on the con-

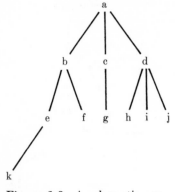

Figure 1.3 A schematic representation of a tree

vention, with either all branches pointed generally downward, as in Figure 1.3, or generally upward.

Definition 1.17:   A *subtree* is a subset of a tree, such that the subset is itself a tree.

Since trees were defined in terms of sets, a subtree can be defined in terms of subsets. Pictorially, it can be viewed as taking some node in the tree and pruning off all of the structure above it and some amount below, leaving another tree structure. Thus, in the tree sample of Figure 1.4, both (a) and (b) are subtrees while the subset in (c) is not a subtree since, although it is a subset, it is not a tree. Similarly the structure in Figure 1.4(d) is not a subtree either since, although it is a tree, it is not a subset of the original tree.

Notice the resemblance to a family tree or the pedigree of your family dog (if he has one). Some of the nomenclature for trees and parts of trees derives from this resemblance. For example, consider the small tree in Figure 1.5 with a as its root. The root is called the *ancestor* of nodes b, c, and d since it is at the tail of the directed branch from a to all three of those points. Similarly, node d is the ancestor of node e. Nodes b, c, and d, on the other hand, are called *descendants* of a, and they are *siblings* of each other.

There are two other tree concepts that will appear continually in the book.

Definition 1.18:   A *binary tree* is a tree in which each node has at most two descendants.

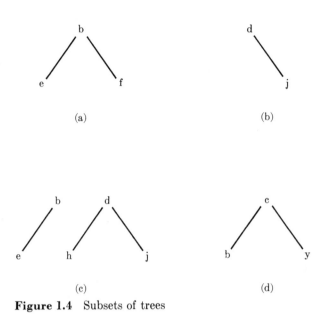

Figure 1.4 Subsets of trees

There are programming advantages to binary trees in machines in which a data word length is twice the length of the address field, a common structure. However, binary trees also clearly illustrate some of the concepts behind translation (to be presented later).

Definition 1.19:   An *oriented tree* is a tree in which, for every node, all descendants from a node are ordered with respect to each other.

If a, b, and c are descendants of a node g in an oriented tree, they form an ordered set. This order is indicated in the schematic representations by assuming that the nodes are in order from left to right. Thus while the diagrams in Figure 1.6 represent the same tree by the general definition of trees, they represent different oriented

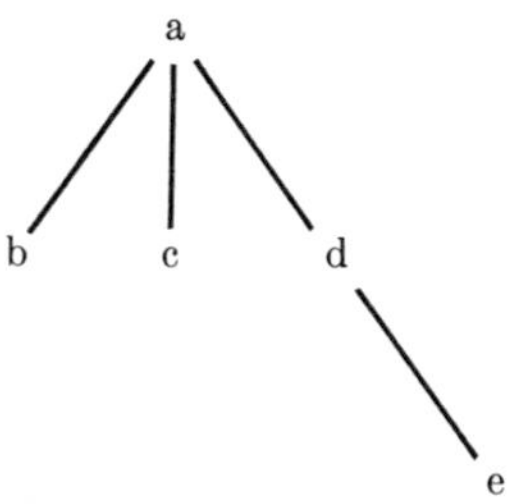

Figure 1.5   A small tree

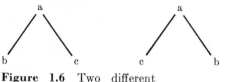

Figure 1.6 Two different oriented trees

trees. All trees in this book will be assumed to be oriented unless otherwise stated.

1.7   *walks of trees*

Later it will be shown that the translation of a sentence results in a representation of it as a tree, analogous to the process of diagramming a sentence in English. To generate machine code, or directly execute the sentence, the compiler must examine each node of the tree in a predetermined order. This ordered examination of the nodes of a tree is called *walking* the tree.

Definition 1.20: A *walk* of a tree is an ordered sequence of nodes of the tree, each node appearing exactly once.

Given any tree, any arbitrary sequence of the nodes is a walk, according to the definition. However, algorithms for generating the walks systematically are necessary so that the computer can develop predictable and reproducible nodal sequences. There are many such algorithms, only a few of which are useful (or, at least, used). Two of the useful ones will be discussed here.

Both walk procedures view any tree as a root with a sequence of subtrees below it, as shown in Figure 1.7. In some cases, the

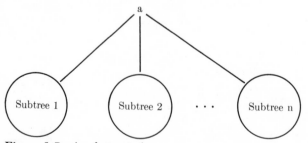

Figure 1.7 An abstract view of an oriented tree

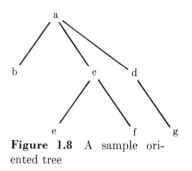

Figure 1.8 A sample oriented tree

subtree may, in fact, be a single node; that is, a root with no descendants. The tree in Figure 1.8 has the subtrees shown in Figure 1.9. Of
course, the subtrees are trees themselves and so can again be viewed
as roots with descendant subtrees. The procedures below make use
of this *nesting* property.

Algorithm: Preorder Walk

Step 1: Visit the root.

Step 2: Visit each subtree successively from left to right, in preorder.

Algorithm: Postorder Walk

Step 1: Visit each subtree successively from left to right, in
postorder.

Step 2: Visit the root.

The names of the algorithms are suggestive. In the preorder
walk, the root is visited first; in the postorder walk, the root is visited

b

Subtree 1   Subtree 2   Subtree 3

Figure 1.9 Subtrees of sample
tree of Figure 1.8

after the subtrees. The walks of the sample tree in Figure 1.8 are as follows.

Preorder Walk: abcefdg

Postorder Walk: befcgda

problems

1. Write the formal description for the following sets: (a) all positive integers between but not equal to 1 and 5; (b) all negative integers, (c) all English words; (d) all textbooks you are using in this course.

2. Let
$$\Sigma = \{a, b, c\}$$
$$T = \{c, d, e\}$$
$$\Phi = \{f, c\}$$

    Calculate the following sets

    (a) $\Sigma \cup T$

    (b) $\Phi - \Sigma$

    (c) $\Sigma \cap T$

    (d) $(T - \Phi) \cap \Sigma$

3. Assume that the sets are defined as in the above problem and state whether the following propositions are true.

    (a) $\Sigma \supset T$

    (b) $(\Sigma \cap T) \subset \Sigma$

    (c) $(\Phi \cap T) = (\Phi \cap \Sigma)$

4. Let $\bar{a}$ and $\bar{b}$ be strings, and $\cdot$ be the concatenation operator.   Is it true that
$$\bar{a} \cdot \bar{b} = \bar{b} \cdot \bar{a}$$

5. Show that
$$\Sigma^n = \Sigma \cdot \Sigma^{n-1} = \Sigma^{n-1} \cdot \Sigma$$

6. In general, is it true for any sets Σ and T that
$$\Sigma \cdot T = T \cdot \Sigma$$

    Prove it or provide a counterexample.

7. Show that
$$|\bar{a}\bar{b}| = |\bar{a}| + |\bar{b}|$$

8. Show that, as stated in Section 1.4, $\bar{a} \in \Sigma^n$ implies that $|\bar{a}| = n$. Hint: Try an inductive proof.

9. Describe, or characterize, the following sets.

    (a) $\{a\}^*$

    (b) $\{b\} \cdot \{a\}^*$

    (c) $\{b\}^* \cdot \{a\}^*$

10. Let a graph be defined as follows.

    $\Sigma = \{a, b, c, d, e, f\}$
    $\Phi = \{\{a, d\}, \{a, e\}, \{b, c\}, \{b, d\}, \{d, f\}\}$

    Are the following pairs of nodes connected?

    (a) $\{c, e\}$

    (b) $\{d, a\}$

    (c) $\{c, f\}$

    (d) $\{f, e\}$

11. Are the following directed graphs trees?

    (a) $\Sigma = \{a, b, c\}$
       $\Phi = \{(a, b)\}$

    (b) $\Sigma = \{a, b, c\}$
       $\Phi = \{(a, b), (b, c), (c, d)\}$

    (c) $\Sigma = \{a, b, c, d\}$
       $\Phi = \{(a, b), (a, c), (b, c), (b, d), (c, d)\}$

12. Draw a sketch of the following tree.

    $\Sigma = \{a, b, c, d, e, f\}$
    $\Phi = \{\{a, b\}, \{a, c\}, \{a, d\}, \{d, e\}, \{d, f\}\}$

    Describe the relationship between the following pairs of points: (a) a to d; (b) f to d; (c) f to e.

13. Show that every node in a tree is connected to the root by one and only one path.

14. Find the preorder and postorder walks of the trees defined in Problem 12.

2

translation of arithmetic expressions

The algebraic language of arithmetic is a simple model of a computer language, and study of its translation will illustrate many of the problems and techniques employed in dealing with more complex languages. Arithmetic expressions are an important part of most computer languages, so translation of them is a part of the compiler's job. Thus arithmetic expressions are both a part of and a model of complex computer languages. A view of the historical development of techniques for compiling arithmetic expressions will show how the science of compiling has evolved toward formalization and the development of a theoretical basis for improving algorithms.

By *compiling* is meant the derivation of consecutive operations that will terminate with the value of the arithmetic expression, provided the value of each variable is known. No distinction is made at this stage between *constant* and *unknown variables*. They both bear the name *operand*. In the same way it is of no concern whether the compilation process calculates as it proceeds or stores the steps for later execution.

The algorithms that follow use the word *scans*. Assuming that the compiler reads the expression linearly, a *scan*, or *pass*, is a complete reading of the input string. Algorithms are characterized as *one pass*, *two pass*, and so on.

2.1   the triplet

Nearly all algebraic operations are binary. Thus a useful concept is the algebraic *triplet* of elements, consisting of the two operands and the result.

$$E_C = E_L \odot E_R$$

where E_C = result
E_L = left-hand operand
$\odot$ = operator
E_R = right-hand operand

Unary operations, such as negation, can be considered to be special cases of binary operations, where E_L is assumed to have a special value and plays no role in the calculation. For example, if the negation operator is used, $\odot$ would be subtraction and $E_L = 0$. The translator's task, given an expression, is to find a sequence (not necessarily unique) of triplet operations that, when executed with the values of the variables defined, calculates the value of that expression.

Many of the intermediate triplets in the calculation will not require the result E_C to be stored in a variable location; instead it will be held as an intermediate value. The notation T_i $(i = 1, \ldots)$ is used to represent temporary variables not declared or used in the program itself, but defined and used by the translator during its processing. For example,

$$d = a + b \times c$$

is calculated by first finding the value of $b \times c$ and then adding a to that result. The set of triplets is

$$T_1 = b \times c$$
$$d = a + T_1$$

The temporary variable T_1 does not have to be stored in memory; it can be held in a register, ready for use in the next calculation. Since the number of temporary variables is unknown in advance, a sophisticated translator will optimize the use of temporary storage during execution. For example, the expression

$$g = ((a + b) \times c \uparrow d + e \times f)$$

could be evaluated by the following string of triplets

$$T_1 = a + b$$
$$T_2 = c \uparrow d$$
$$T_3 = T_1 \times T_2$$
$$T_4 = e \times f$$
$$g = T_3 + T_4$$

However, a more optimum use of temporary storage would be the use of the following sequence of triplets.

$$T_1 = a + b$$
$$T_2 = c \uparrow d$$
$$T_1 = T_1 \times T_2$$
$$T_2 = e \times f$$
$$g = T_1 + T_2$$

If the machine had only two high-speed registers available, the latter calculation might be much faster than the former, saving 4 memory accesses out of 11. If this expression were in a loop, cycling thousands of times, a nearly 40 percent saving in time would be significant.

2.2   early methods

Some of the earliest developments toward higher-order computer languages were systems allowing scientists to describe numerical calculations in the form of algebraic expressions.   Many early users of computers were scientists calculating the solutions to complex equations. Systems were designed that allowed the users to write their formulas directly in a convenient form for them, and that translated these formulas into machine-language code.   In fact, FORTRAN was one of these early systems and was named from a contraction of the words FORmula TRANslator.

Control of temporary storage and the decisions of precedence were the two major problems facing the designers of algebraic-expression translators in those days.   When were temporary variables needed, and how were they used when evaluating an expression?   Given an expression as a string of operators and operands, what operation was to be performed first?   These questions were not trivial to the system designers of that day, and either very complex algorithms were written to take care of them, or simplifications and restrictions on the form of the expression were set.

For example, in one of the earliest algorithms, due to Rutishauser, the expressions were assumed to be fully parenthesized and no implicit precedence of operators was assumed.   So the formula

$$a + b \times c$$

was illegal. The precedence rule requiring that the multiplication be performed first in the above expression was to be shown explicitly by parentheses.

$$a + (b \times c)$$

Incidentally, the circle has turned fully in this matter, since APL once again observes no implicit precedence among operators. The reasons for this rule relate to the philosophy of the language rather than the problems of translation, and there is a default interpretation. If no precedence is specified by parentheses, the expression is evaluated from right to left. Thus

$$a + b \times c$$

would be evaluated as custom would expect, but

$$b \times c + a$$

would be evaluated by calculating $c + a$ first and then multiplying the result by b.

Given the fully parenthesized expression, Rutishauser's algorithm assigned to each symbol S_i in the string a number M_i according to the following algorithm, in which $S(J)$ is the j-th symbol and $N(J)$ is the j-th number. The variable $NMAX$ contains the largest value of N assigned.

Algorithm: Assign

Assign 1: $N(0) \leftarrow 0; J \leftarrow 0;$

Assign 2: $J \leftarrow J + 1;$ **If** done **Then** $N(J) \leftarrow 0$ and **Exit;**

Assign 3:   **If** $S(J)$ is a (or an operand **Then** $N(J) \leftarrow N(J - 1) + 1;$
             Go to *Assign 2;*

Assign 4: $N(J) \leftarrow N(J - 1) - 1;$
             Go to *Assign 2;*

The first symbol $S(0)$ represents the space just before the actual string starts. Note that the final value of J is 1 more than the string length. For example, given the following phrase

$$a + (b \times c)$$

the numbering would be as follows.

$$
\begin{array}{lccccccccc}
J: & 0 & 1 & 2 & 3 & 4 & 5 & 6 & 7 & 8 \\
S(J): & & a & + & (& b & \times & c &) & \\
N(J): & 0 & 1 & 0 & 1 & 2 & 1 & 2 & 1 & 0
\end{array}
$$

The translator, then, searches for the largest value of N. This value, call it k, appears paired in a structure of the form

$$
N(J): \quad \cdots \ (k-1) \quad k \quad (k-1) \quad k \quad (k-1) \ \cdots
$$

Of course, more than one of these structures could appear in the expression, but that does not matter. The translator merely takes the first one it finds. The structure corresponds to a sequence of symbols of the following form.

$$
\mathcal{L} \quad \text{operand}_1 \quad \mathcal{O} \quad \text{operand}_2 \quad \mathcal{R}
$$

The symbol $\mathcal{L}$ is either a left parenthesis or the left end of the expression. Similarly, $\mathcal{R}$ is the right parenthesis or the right end of the expression. The symbol $\mathcal{O}$ represents an operator. When the structure is found, the points are *pounded down* by calculating the value of the binary expression and storing it in a temporary location T_i. The triplet

$$
T_i \leftarrow \text{operand}_1 \quad \mathcal{O} \quad \text{operand}_2
$$

is formed. The three symbols are deleted along with $\mathcal{L}$ and $\mathcal{R}$ if they are parentheses, and T_i is put in their place with the value $N = (k-1)$. If $\mathcal{L}$ and $\mathcal{R}$ are the ends of the string, the process is completed. Otherwise the algorithm repeats its search for the largest number N. The example above, if processed one step, becomes

$$
\begin{array}{lccccc}
S(J): & & a & + & T_i & \\
N(J): & 0 & 1 & 0 & 1 & 0
\end{array}
$$

Of course, the restriction of requiring parentheses is severe, and preprocessors were designed to insert them. A translator written for FORTRAN II on an IBM 704 inserted parentheses and other special indicator marks with abandon. In one example, the arithmetic expression was 15 symbols long (including the end-of-string markers). The final string, after all insertions had been made, was **87** characters long!

A more elaborate example of Rutishauser's method is worked out completely below.

Generated Triplet	*Expression*
	$(((a + b) \times c) + d) \div (e + (a \div f))$ 01234 3 43 2 32 1 21 0 12 1 23 2 3210
$T_1 = a + b$	$((T_1 \times c) + d) \div (e + (a \div f))$ 0123 2 32 1 21 0 12 1 23 2 3210
$T_1 = T_1 \times c$	$(T_1 + d) \div (e + (a \div f))$ 012 1 21 0 12 1 12 2 3210
$T_2 = a \div f$	$(T_1 + d) \div (e + T_2)$ 012 1 21 0 12 1 2 10
$T_1 = T_1 + d$	$T_1 \div (e + T_2)$ 01 0 12 1 2 10
$T_2 = e + T_2$	$T_1 \div T_2$ 01 0 1 0
$T_1 = T_1 \div T_2$	

2.3   stack techniques

An important technique for analyzing arithmetic expressions was introduced by Bauer and Samelson; this technique will appear in a different guise later in this book. The technique makes use of the push-down stack, or *cellar,* as they called it at that time, and of a *transition table.* The push-down stack has been discussed in Chapter 1; transition tables will be discussed here.

The analyzer uses two push-down stacks. One stack is used directly as it translates the expression, and the other is used during execution. The translator stack is labeled T and the execution stack is labeled E. The translator reads the expression once, from left to right, and outputs a sequence of instructions of two forms:

K_I (where I is an identifier) is the instruction "Take the number whose name is I and put it on the stack E."

K_ξ (where ξ is an operator) is the instruction "Take the top two operands from the stack E, operate on them with ξ, and store the result on top of the stack E."

In scanning the input string, if the symbol read is an operand I, the instruction K_I is output and the translator moves on to the next symbol. If the symbol read is an operator ξ, one of several actions is taken. Usually, either ξ is pushed on T or the instruction K_ξ is output. The transition table is used to direct the translator to the appropriate action. This table has rows and columns corresponding to the operators in the language. The entries of the table contain the directions to the translator. There are four possible actions to be taken by the translator after reading an operator, ξ. (The operator on top of T is designated by η.)

I: Push ξ on T; Read next symbol.

II: Generate K_η; Push ξ on T; Read next symbol.

III: Pop T; Read next symbol (used to delete parenthesis).

IV: Generate K_η; Pop T; Repeat with same input symbols.

There are two other special instructions, *End of Process* and *Error*, which instruct the translator to stop and output the proper instruction. The processor reads the table using as one index η, the top operator in T, and, as the second, ξ, the operator last read off the input string. The table in Figure 2.1 is used for a simple arithmetic expression language. In the table, Λ stands for the blank symbol, or empty

ξ = input symbol

		Λ	(	+	−	×	/	)
	Λ	End	I	I	I	I	I	Error
	(	Error	I	I	I	II	II	III
η = top of stack T	+	IV	I	II	II	I	I	IV
	−	IV	I	II	II	I	I	IV
	×	IV	I	IV	IV	II	II	IV
	/	IV	I	IV	IV	II	II	IV

Figure 2.1 A transition table
for simple algebraic expressions

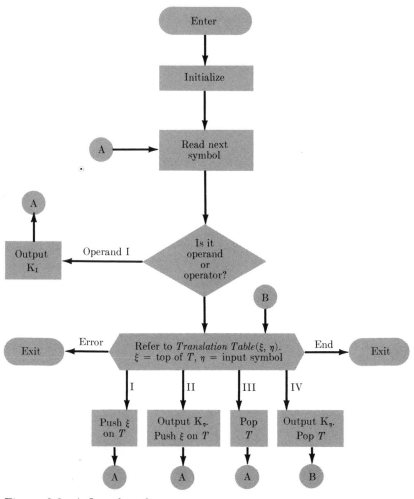

Figure 2.2   A flow chart for push-down translator

string. If the stack T is empty, Λ is considered to have been read. Similarly, if the input string is empty, Λ will be considered read. Figure 2.2 shows a flow chart for the push-down translator.

Let us apply this processor to an expression and see how it works. The expression is

$$(a \times b + c \times d)/(a - d) + b \times c$$

The sequence of steps in processing it is shown below.

T	Input Symbol Read	Action	Instruction Output
Λ	)	I	
(	a		K_a
(	$\times$	I	
($\times$	b		K_b
($\times$	+	IV	$K_\times$
(	Repeat	I	
(+	c		K_c
(+	$\times$	I	
(+$\times$	d		K_d
(+$\times$	)	IV	$K_\times$
(+	Repeat	IV	K_+
(	Repeat	III	
Λ	/	I	
/	(	I	
/(	a		K_a
/(	$-$	I	
/($-$	d		K_d
/($-$	)	IV	K_-
/(	Repeat	III	
/	+	IV	$K_/$
Λ	Repeat	I	
+	b		K_b
+	$\times$	I	
+$\times$	c		K_c
+$\times$	Λ	IV	$K_\times$
+	Λ	IV	K_+
Λ	Λ	End	

The instruction sequence is

$$K_a,\ K_b,\ K_\times,\ K_c,\ K_d,\ K_\times,\ K_+,\ K_a,\ K_d,\ K_-,\ K_/,\ K_b,\ K_c,\ K_\times,\ K_+$$

However, a simpler representation results from dropping the K's.

$$ab \times cd \times +\ ad - /bc \times +$$

This simpler representation of the program is a parenthesis-free form that may be familiar to some readers. It is sometimes called the

Polish form, after its developer, the Polish mathematician Lukasie-wicz. The executing program uses a push-down stack E and reads the Polish form from left to right. If it reads an operand, the operand is pushed on E; if an operator, the operator is applied to the top two elements of E. In the form produced by the translator, there are no implicit or explicit problems of precedence. The program is executed directly from left to right. Temporary storage is automatically controlled by use of the push-down stack E, which holds all temporary intermediate values.

problems

1. Show a sequence of triplets that will correctly evaluate the following expressions.

    (a) $(a + b)/(c + d)$

    (b) $a \times b \times c \times d$

    (c) $c \times (a + b)/d$

2. Apply Rutishauser's method to the three expressions in Problem 1. Display the intermediate steps as in the text.

3. In Rutishauser's method, why must the end symbols $\mathcal{L}$ and $\mathcal{R}$ in a peak structure both be parentheses or both be end-of-string symbols?

4. Modify the *Assign* algorithm to make identification of the highest peaks possible without a complete scan during translation.

5. Show that the highest peak, k, must occur paired in a structure of the form $(k - 1)k(k - 1)k(k - 1)$.

6. Assume that there is a function, *Precedence* $(\mathcal{O}_1, \mathcal{O}_2)$, available that, given the two operators $\mathcal{O}_1$ and $\mathcal{O}_2$ as arguments, will furnish the relative precedence between them. Use the function to write an algorithm that will insert the parentheses in an arithmetic expression.

7. Why doesn't the transition table in Figure 2.1 need a row corresponding to the right parenthesis?

8. What do the two *Error* entries in the table say is wrong about the input string?

9. Write the Polish form for the following expressions.

(*a*) (a × b + c) × d × (e/f)

(*b*) a + b + c + d

10. Write a program that will calculate the value of an expression written in Polish form. (This program, in a sense, simulates another computer, a pseudo-computer or pseudo-machine. The Bauer and Samelson translator translates an algebraic expression into machine language for this pseudo-machine, rather than translating into machine language in general. This process of defining a pseudo-machine for the target language is common, especially for more sophisticated languages. If the output is a sequence of instructions in the pseudo-language, which are later interpreted by another program during execution time, the compiler is *interpretive* in nature. Alternatively, the pseudo-instructions output from the translator could be reconstituted into sequences of real machine-language operations later in the compilation process.)

11. Write a push-down translator that will output the Polish form of an algebraic expression, given the transition table shown in Figure 2.1.

12. Extend the translation table to allow for a new operator ↑, the *exponential* operator, that is, a ↑ b = a^b.

13. Discuss how the translator and the transition table could be modified to accommodate the unary negation operator.

3
formal models of
grammars

In order to develop algorithms for translating languages, a theoretical model of grammars is necessary. We will develop such a model in this chapter. The model will define a way for formally describing grammars, and will propose a process for building sentences from these descriptions.

The entire theory of formal languages, of which the following is only a simple beginning, can be quite complex mathematically and it is a powerful tool for the study of languages and computers. In a sense it stands between the pragmatic art of writing compilers on one side and automata theory on the other. Thus its importance and utility are far beyond the scope of this book. At the same time, as is usually the case with mathematical models, it is not a complete description of language, not even computer languages. The most obvious deficiency in this regard is that the theory is concerned only with the formal structure or *syntax* of a sentence, as opposed to the meaning or *semantic* content of the sentence.

3.1 *syntax and semantics*

The simple distinction between syntax and semantics is important to understand at this point. The syntax of a language is a set of rules for assembling its basic symbols—*words*—into sentences. The semantics of a language is the set of rules for interpreting the meaning of a sentence. This meaning will depend on the specific words chosen, the syntactic structure of the sentence, and, often, the context of the sentence. The distinction is simple only at this level; the concepts become hopelessly entangled in advanced linguistic theory, which we will not need here.

For example, suppose you are told that "boc" is a singular noun, "trag" a verb, and "snuvley" an adverb, all in the English language. Then you can presume that "The boc trags snuvley" is an English sentence, even though the meaning is somewhat obscure. But, after all, new words are invented every day, and we usually do not need to learn an additional grammatical rule for each new word. Generally, the rules that govern how a sentence is put together remain unchanged over the short term although the words change. In this sense, the syntax of a language is considered to be independent of the meaning. However, the reverse is not true. That is, the meaning is quite dependent on the syntax. Even in the nonsense sentence above, we know that a "boc," whatever it is, is "tragging" (note that we even have standard rules to transform a nonsense verb in tense or case), and it is doing it "snuvley," as one might hope. This dependence of meaning on syntax is reminiscent of Alice's comment after she hears the tale of the Jabberwock, ". . . Somebody killed something; that's clear, at any rate."

Neither the model described in this chapter, nor any other developed to date, is broad enough to include a full description of a natural language such as English. Whether such a model can even be built is the subject of a great deal of debate. A model could be constructed that would produce only proper English sentences, but, of course, that is not the same as producing all English sentences. And remember, since semantics depends on syntax, merely producing proper English sentences is not enough—they must be produced by rules of syntax that allow the semantics of the sentence to be unscrambled. However, the model described below is useful in treating the translation and design of computer languages.

3.2   *terminal symbols and syntactic variables*

The basic elements out of which strings or sentences are constructed are called the *terminal symbols* of the language. In natural language, these are words or pieces of words. Notice that, since a word is usually made up of more than one character or letter, the word *symbol* as used here does not necessarily imply a single character, but rather represents a group of letters assembled to form the terminal symbol.

In the English language, **that, dog,** and **cow,** not the individual letters that make up the words, are terminal symbols. The sentence

Cow, bite that dog!

is made up of four terminal symbols, if the punctuation is not considered as part of the grammar (six terminal symbols if the comma and exclamation point are included). They are **Cow, bite, that,** and **dog.**

Various number representations can also be considered to be sentences in special languages. For example, in the decimal system, integers are built by using the 10 digits. In this case, the symbols are one character long. For example, the number **6240** is composed of four terminal symbols, **6, 2, 4,** and **0.**

Since, in general, terminal symbols may be more than one character long, the translator program in the computer may require a routine between it and the input. This routine, called a *preprocessor,* in its simplest form reads the input string, recognizes the multicharacter terminal symbols, and passes on to the translator a single internal representation of the symbol. For example, the verb **Go to** that appears in many programming languages is a single operator, just as much as $+$, even though it takes up five places on the input string. The preprocessor reads the five characters and passes on to the translator the single internal operator symbol standing for **Go to.**

The preprocessor itself may be a syntax-oriented translator. The names of operands, for example, can be constructed out of basic alphabetic and numeric characters according to fixed syntactic rules. The preprocessor can then translate these operand names according to the rules, set up tables, and pass on to the translator only the single internal character standing for that operand. Thus the terminal-symbol set used by the translator is not always the same terminal-symbol set we use when we write a program.

Why stage syntax translation this way? The reasons will become clearer later in the book. Basically, some syntactic models allow for more efficient translating algorithms than others. If the syntax describing operand names, for example, is such a simpler model, much efficiency can be gained by translating operands via that simpler model rather than by the much more complex model needed for the full language.

In the following pages, terminal symbols are represented by capital Latin letters or boldface words. The symbols A and **word** are terminal symbols. The symbol Σ designates a set of terminal symbols.

The concept of a variable ranging over a set of values is a useful tool in most mathematical theories, including the formalism being developed. So, *syntactic variables* are introduced here. They will be represented by lowercase Greek letters, and a set of syntactic variables will be labeled T. A lowercase Latin letter will represent any symbol, terminal or variable.

There is, however, another notation for syntactic variables that is useful in discussing languages. It is often convenient and easier for the reader if specific variables can be named, that is, designated by a form more suggestive of their intuitive meaning. The form used for this purpose is to simply enclose the name, in italics, with a pair of angular brackets ⟨ and ⟩. For example, in English, the syntactic variables are the *parts of speech*. Thus ⟨*noun*⟩ is a syntactic variable ranging over a particular set of words (terminal symbols), including the word **noun** itself. Basically, syntactic variables are symbols that do not appear in the final sentence, but that take part in the definition of the grammar and the construction of the sentence.

3.3   synthesizing strings

The parts of speech occur in descriptions of English when rules are formed for constructing sentences. For instance, a grammar might state that a ⟨*sentence*⟩ can be constructed from a ⟨*plural noun*⟩ followed by a ⟨*verb*⟩. (To be completely precise, of course, the case and tense of the verb would have to be specified.) Thus if **aardvarks** is a ⟨*plural noun*⟩, and **fly** is a ⟨*verb*⟩, then **aardvarks fly** is a ⟨*sentence*⟩ according to the above definition.

The fundamental purpose of a grammar is to describe how to construct strings of terminal symbols, which are the *sentence*s of the language. The fundamental operation for this construction is a *substitution*. Suppose we have a string with a syntactic variable appearing somewhere in it. The substitution operation would replace that variable in the string with a substring associated with that variable. This operation is represented by the notation

$$\xi \rightarrow \bar{x}$$

Here ξ is a syntactic variable, and $\bar{x}$ is a string of symbols, terminal, variable, or both. The expression above is referred to as a *production*, and can be thought of as a formal substitution rule that can be applied to a string in which the variable ξ occurs.

Suppose we have the strings

$$\bar{y} = A\xi B$$
$$\bar{x} = C\gamma$$

Then the substitution rule can be used to apply the production above to the string $\bar{y}$ to obtain a new string

$$\bar{y} = AC\gamma B$$

As another example, take the ⟨**Go to** *statement*⟩ as a syntactic variable in a simple programming language. Such a variable is constructed by attaching a statement label to the right of the command **Go to.** As mentioned above, **Go to** can be considered to be a single terminal symbol in the language. Since there are many possible statement labels in an interesting language, a new syntactic variable, ⟨*statement label*⟩, is introduced, and the construction rule can be expressed in the form of the following production

$$\langle \textbf{Go to } statement \rangle \rightarrow \textbf{Go to } \langle statement\ label \rangle \qquad (3.1)$$

Now suppose that all statement labels in this simple programming language must be four-digit numbers with the letter A on the left. For example, A1001 is a statement label. Then ⟨*four-digit number*⟩ can be considered to be another variable, and the rule for constructing a statement label can be expressed in the following form.

$$\langle statement\ label \rangle \rightarrow A \langle four\text{-}digit\ number \rangle \qquad (3.2)$$

The right-hand side of Expression (3.1), after the substitution indicated by Expression (3.2), becomes

$$\textbf{Go to } A \langle four\text{-}digit\ number \rangle \qquad (3.3)$$

This type of single substitution is designated by a double arrow $\Rightarrow$, and the left-hand string is said to *directly produce* the right-hand string. The operation described just above can be expressed in the following manner.

$$\textbf{Go to } \langle statement\ label \rangle \Rightarrow \textbf{Go to } A \langle four\text{-}digit\ number \rangle$$

If one string is created from another by one or more substitutions, a starred arrow $\overset{*}{\Rightarrow}$ is used. In this case, the left-hand string is said to *produce* the right-hand string. For example, Expressions (3.2) and (3.3) can be put together to form

$$\langle \textbf{Go to } statement \rangle \Rightarrow \textbf{Go to } \langle statement\ label \rangle$$
$$\Rightarrow \textbf{Go to } A \langle four\text{-}digit\ number \rangle$$

The expression above can be contracted, if the intermediate results are not important to express explicitly, to the following form:

$$\langle \textbf{Go to } \textit{statement} \rangle \stackrel{*}{\Rightarrow} \textbf{Go to } \text{A } \langle \textit{four-digit number} \rangle$$

There may be more than one production with the same left-hand side. Suppose labels are allowed that are four-digit numbers preceded by a B. Now there are two productions defining a statement label.

$$\langle \textit{statement label} \rangle \rightarrow \text{A } \langle \textit{four-digit number} \rangle$$

and
$$\langle \textit{statement label} \rangle \rightarrow \text{B } \langle \textit{four-digit number} \rangle$$

Either production can be used to substitute for the variable $\langle \textit{statement label} \rangle$ where it appears in a string. This set of productions could also have been expressed in the following manner.

$$\langle \textit{statement label} \rangle \rightarrow \langle \textit{letter} \rangle \langle \textit{four-digit number} \rangle$$
$$\langle \textit{letter} \rangle \rightarrow \text{A}$$
$$\langle \textit{letter} \rangle \rightarrow \text{B}$$

These three productions produce by substitution the same strings that the previous set produced. Thus the following expressions hold.

$$\langle \textit{statement label} \rangle \stackrel{*}{\Rightarrow} \text{A } \langle \textit{four-digit number} \rangle$$

and
$$\langle \textit{statement label} \rangle \stackrel{*}{\Rightarrow} \text{B } \langle \textit{four-digit number} \rangle$$

Notice from the above example that given any language, there may be a multiplicity of grammars that generate it. If there are two different grammars G_1 and G_2 which generate identical sets of sentences G_1 and G_2 are said to be *equivalent*.

3.4   definition of grammars

We will now formalize the concepts introduced above. Remember from Chapter 1 that the asterisk operation on a set indicates the set consisting of all finite-length strings of elements in the set, including the string of zero length, the empty string ε. Let Σ again be a set of terminal symbols, and let T be a set of variable symbols.

Definition 3.1:   A *production* is an ordered pair of strings $(\bar{x}, \bar{y})$ where $\bar{x} \in \{T^* - \varepsilon\}$ and $\bar{y} \in (T \cup \Sigma)^*$. The production can be written

$$\bar{x} \rightarrow \bar{y}$$

The left-hand string is called the *root* of the production, and the right-hand string is called the *argument* of the production.

Notice that the null string ε can appear on the right-hand side but not on the left-hand side of the production. A grammar G can now be defined as follows:

Definition 3.2: A *phrase-structure grammar* (PSG) is an ordered quadruple

$$G = (\Sigma, T, \Pi, \sigma)$$

where Σ = set of terminal symbols

 T = set of variable symbols

 Π = indexed set of productions in Σ and T

 σ = variable symbol in T such that $\sigma \rightarrow \bar{y}$ is a production in Π for some string $\bar{y}$. σ is called the *starting symbol* of the grammar.

Below are some examples of PSG's and non-PSG's:

1. $(\Sigma = \{A, B\}, T = \{\alpha, \beta, \gamma\}, \Pi = \{\alpha \rightarrow ABA, \alpha\beta \rightarrow B, \beta \rightarrow B\alpha\}, \alpha)$ is a PSG.
2. $(\Sigma = \{A, B\}, T = \{\alpha, \beta, \gamma\}, \Pi = \{\alpha \rightarrow ABA, \alpha\beta \rightarrow B, B \rightarrow B\alpha, \alpha \rightarrow \epsilon\}, \alpha)$ is not a PSG, for one of the productions violates the requirement that the left-hand string be an element of T^*.

Two of the concepts introduced in Section 3.3 can now be more rigorously defined.

Definition 3.3: Let $\bar{x}$ and $\bar{y}$ be arbitrary strings of terminal and variable symbols [$\bar{x}$ and $\bar{y} \in (\Sigma \cup T)^*$], where $\bar{x}$ is not the empty string ($\bar{x} \neq \epsilon$). Then $\bar{x}$ *directly produces* $\bar{y}$ ($\bar{x} \Rightarrow \bar{y}$) if and only if $\bar{x}$ contains a substring $\bar{\omega}_2$

$$\bar{x} = \bar{\omega}_1\bar{\omega}_2\bar{\omega}_3$$

such that ω_2 is the root of a production

$$\bar{\omega}_2 \rightarrow \bar{z}$$

in Π, and $\bar{y}$ is the result of substituting $\bar{z}$ for $\bar{\omega}_2$

$$\bar{y} = \bar{\omega}_1\bar{z}\bar{\omega}_2$$

Definition 3.4: Let $\bar{x}$ and $\bar{y}$ be strings defined as in Definition 3.3. Then $\bar{x}$ *produces* $\bar{y}$ ($\bar{x} \overset{*}{\Rightarrow} \bar{y}$) if and only if there exists a set of strings $\bar{z}_1, \bar{z}_2, \ldots, \bar{z}_n$ (for $n > 2$) such that the following conditions hold:

$$\bar{z}_1 = \bar{x}$$
$$\bar{z}_n = \bar{y}$$

and $\quad\quad \bar{z}_i \Rightarrow \bar{z}_{i+1} \quad$ for all $i = 1, 2, \ldots, n - 1$

That is, there is a sequence of one or more direct productions from $\bar{x}$ to $\bar{y}$, or

$$x = \bar{z}_1 \Rightarrow \bar{z}_2 \Rightarrow \bar{z}_3 \cdots \bar{z}_n = \bar{y}$$

Examples: In the following examples

$$G = (\{A, B, C\}, \{\alpha, \beta, \gamma, \sigma\}, \Pi, \sigma)$$

where

$$
\begin{aligned}
\Pi = \{ &\sigma \to \alpha\beta & &:1 \\
&\alpha \to AB & &:2 \\
&\beta\gamma \to \alpha & &:3 \\
&\beta \to C & &:4\}
\end{aligned}
$$

The numbers on the right of the productions are their indices, used to identify them uniquely.   From the production set the following statements hold.

(a) $\qquad\qquad\qquad A\alpha C \overset{2}{\Rightarrow} AABC$

(Occasionally, to illustrate more clearly how a direct production is generated, the index of the production used is put over the $\Rightarrow$ and the variable used as the root of the substitution is underlined.)

(b) $\qquad\qquad\qquad \underline{\beta\gamma}\alpha \overset{3}{\Rightarrow} \alpha\alpha$

(c) The expression $\qquad \beta\gamma\alpha \overset{*}{\Rightarrow} ABAB$

compresses the sequence

$$\underline{\beta\gamma}\alpha \overset{3}{\Rightarrow} \underline{\alpha}\alpha \overset{2}{\Rightarrow} AB\underline{\alpha} \overset{2}{\Rightarrow} ABAB$$

But expression (c) can also be generated by the sequences

$$\underline{\beta\gamma}\alpha \overset{3}{\Rightarrow} \alpha\underline{\alpha} \overset{2}{\Rightarrow} \underline{\alpha}AB \overset{2}{\Rightarrow} ABAB$$

and $\qquad\quad \beta\underline{\gamma\alpha} \overset{2}{\Rightarrow} \underline{\beta\gamma}AB \overset{3}{\Rightarrow} \underline{\alpha}AB \overset{2}{\Rightarrow} ABAB$

Thus $\bar{x} \overset{*}{\Rightarrow} \bar{y}$ does not necessarily imply a unique sequence of productions involved.   In fact, the first two sequences use the same order of application for the productions 3, 2, and 2, and still form two different transformation sequences.   So the order of application of the productions is not even sufficient to define uniquely a production sequence.   This idea will be explored in more detail later, but now it is time to look at languages themselves.

The definition of a language follows directly from the definition of a grammar.   In fact, a language is merely a set (not necessarily finite) of strings of terminal symbols constructed according to rules established by the grammar.

Definition 3.5: Let $G = (\Sigma, T, \Pi, \sigma)$ be a PSG. The *language* of G is the set Λ of strings of terminal symbols ($\Lambda \subset \Sigma^*$) such that a string $\bar{x}$ is in Λ if and only if it is produced by the starting variable σ ($\sigma \overset{*}{\Rightarrow} \bar{x}$). An element of Λ is called a *sentence* of the language.

A generalization of the sentence will also be useful to us.

Definition 3.6: A *sentential form* $\bar{s}$ of a grammar $G = (\Sigma, T, \Pi, \sigma)$ is a string of terminal and/or variable symbols produced by σ.

$$\bar{s} \in (\Sigma \cup T)^* \qquad \text{and} \qquad \sigma \overset{*}{\Rightarrow} \bar{s}$$

In many of the examples to follow in this chapter and succeeding ones very elementary grammars with few terminal symbols and variables will be used. The production sets will also usually be limited in size. Although these simple languages do not bear much immediate resemblance to programming languages, much less to natural languages, they still are very important. Such simple languages are useful in distilling properties, both good and pathological, of strings produced by phrase-structure grammars. It is difficult to call the set of all finite-length strings of a single letter, say A, a language. Nevertheless, it *is* a language constructed by some grammars of the form defined above. And these grammars exhibit some interesting properties, as will be seen below. This type of experimental grammar is invaluable to computer scientists trying to understand basic properties of abstract languages, and trying on an applied level to devise more efficient compiling techniques.

Below is one of these simple languages. The grammar will produce the set of finite strings of the letter A of odd length.

$$G_1 = (\{A\}, \{\alpha\}, \Pi, \alpha)$$

where

$$\Pi = \{\alpha \rightarrow AA\alpha \qquad :1$$
$$\alpha \rightarrow A \qquad :2\}$$

It is not hard to convince oneself that this grammar indeed produces strings of the type mentioned above. But let us look at a fairly formal argument to see how we could proceed with a more complex case. Assume that the string $\bar{x}$ is in $\Lambda(G)$. Then, by definition, $\alpha \overset{*}{\Rightarrow} \bar{x}$, and there exists a sequence of sentential forms $\bar{z}_1, \bar{z}_2, \ldots, \bar{z}_k$ such that

$$\bar{z}_1 = \alpha$$
$$\bar{z}_k = \bar{x}$$

and $\qquad \bar{z}_i \Rightarrow \bar{z}_{i+1} \qquad$ for $i = 1, 2, \ldots, k-1$

If k = 2, then $\alpha \Rightarrow \bar{x}$ directly. Only production 2 could be involved, and so $\bar{x} = A = \bar{z}_2$. If $k > 2$, then $\bar{z}_2 = AA\alpha$ by production 1. An inductive argument for k will show the following. If

$$\bar{z}_i \Rightarrow \bar{z}_{i+1}$$

and if

$$\bar{z}_i = A^{2m}\alpha$$

then either

$$\bar{z}_{i+1} = A^{2m+2}\alpha$$
or
$$\bar{z}_{i+1} = A^{2m+1}$$

Then, inductively, since

$$\bar{z}_2 = A^2\alpha$$

either

$$\bar{z}_k = A^{2m+2}\alpha$$

for some number m, or

$$\bar{z}_k = A^{2m+1}$$

But $\bar{z}_k$ is a string of terminal characters, so we know it is equal to A^{2m+1} and hence of odd length.

The following grammar of Ginzburg generates strings of A's of length f(n) for n > 1, 2, . . . , where

$$f(n) = \sum_{i=1}^{n} i$$

In a sense it can be called a *generating grammar* for the number f(n).

$$G_G = (\{A\}, \{\alpha, \beta, \gamma, \xi, \mu, \nu, \tau, \sigma\}, \Pi, \sigma)$$

where

$$
\begin{aligned}
\Pi \equiv \{ \sigma &\rightarrow \mu\tau\gamma & &: 1 \\
\gamma &\rightarrow \tau\gamma & &: 2 \\
\gamma &\rightarrow \mu & &: 3 \\
\tau\mu &\rightarrow \xi\alpha & &: 4 \\
\tau\xi &\rightarrow \xi\tau\beta & &: 5 \\
\mu\xi &\rightarrow \mu\nu & &: 6 \\
\nu\tau &\rightarrow \tau\nu & &: 7 \\
\nu\alpha &\rightarrow \mu A & &: 8 \\
\beta\tau &\rightarrow \tau\beta & &: 9 \\
\beta\alpha &\rightarrow \alpha A & &: 10 \\
\mu\mu &\rightarrow \varepsilon & &: 11 \}
\end{aligned}
$$

Showing that this grammar is, indeed, the generating grammar for $f(n)$ is tedious, but it is a straightforward extension of the argument presented above for the first grammar. We assume that $\bar{x} \in \Lambda(G)$, and must show that $\bar{x}$ will have the form $f(n)$ for some n. The major difference in arguments is that in the first it was possible to show a single form for all intermediate sentential forms in the production sequence. In this case, the form changes through the sequence. Also, there are occasionally alternative structures, another problem that does not occur in the simple argument. However, both these problems merely imply greater length and the need for more detailed bookkeeping during the proof. The style of demonstration, the basic form of the proof, remains the same. The argument will be started here, but left to you to finish as a problem.

Let $\bar{x} \in \Lambda(G)$. Then $\sigma \overset{*}{\Rightarrow} \bar{x}$, and there is a sequence of sentential forms $\bar{z}_i$, $i = 1, 2, \ldots, k$, such that $\sigma = \bar{z}_1$, $\bar{x} = \bar{z}_k$, and $\bar{z}_i \Rightarrow \bar{z}_{i+1}$ for $i = 1, 2, \ldots, k - 1$. Now, by production 1

$$\bar{z}_2 = \mu \tau \gamma$$

The next production sequence can only be generated from m applications of production 2, $(m > 0)$ followed by application of production 3. So it is not hard to show that

$$\bar{z}_{3+m} = \mu \tau^{m+1} \qquad m > 1$$

The rest of the argument is left to you.

3.5   *special classes of grammars*

The definition of phrase-structure grammars describes much too large a class of grammars to deal with in the translation process. However, it is possible to define increasingly restricted grammars, with the restrictions often placed on the productions. Naturally, the classes of grammars defined will be less flexible, both in terms of the languages produced and the way the sentences are generated. On the other hand, the restrictions ensure certain properties of the grammars allowing us to study their structure more deeply and develop useful general techniques for translation.

Definition 3.7:   A grammar $G = (\Sigma, T, \Pi, \sigma)$ is called a *context-free grammar* (CFG) if and only if it is a PSG and the roots of all productions $\bar{x} \to \bar{y}$ in Π are single variables ($\bar{x} \in T$). Single productions with this property are referred to as *context-free productions.*

Definition 3.8:   A grammar $G = (\Sigma, T, \Pi, \sigma)$ is called a *context-sensitive grammar* (CSG) if and only if it is a PSG and each production $\bar{x} \to \bar{y}$ in Π is of the following form

$$\bar{x} = \bar{u}_1 \xi \bar{u}_2 \quad \text{and} \quad \bar{y} = \bar{u}_1 \bar{z} \bar{u}_2$$

and $\quad\quad\quad\quad \bar{z} \neq \varepsilon$

Single productions with the above property are called *context-sensitive productions.*

In a context-free grammar, each direct production involves the substitution of a string (possibly empty) for a single variable symbol, specified by the root of the production. In the context-sensitive grammar, the same kind of substitution is made for each direct production; that is, a string (this time specified in the definition as nonempty) is substituted for a single variable. However, the variable must appear in a specified context, $\bar{u}_1$ on the left and $\bar{u}_2$ on the right, which remains unchanged in the substitution. Although the productions appear more restrictive in the context-sensitive grammar, it is a more general class of grammars since most context-free languages are context-sensitive with the contexts $\bar{u}_1$ and $\bar{u}_2$ in each production equal to the empty string ε. The only exception is that context-free grammars with one or more productions having ε as their argument are not context-sensitive grammars.

Suppose, for example, we have two productions

$$\xi \to A \quad\quad :1$$

and $\quad\quad\quad\quad \xi\alpha \to A\alpha \quad :2$

According to the definitions above, production 1 is context-free and production 2 is context-sensitive. Let us apply them to the string

$$B\xi\alpha C$$

Both productions generate the same result, an effective substitution

$$B\xi\alpha C \overset{1}{\Rightarrow} BA\alpha C$$
$$B\xi\alpha C \overset{2}{\Rightarrow} BA\alpha C$$

But while production 1 can be applied to the string

$$B\xi\gamma$$

production 2 cannot be applied. Thus, when the context is proper (in this case the right context is α, the left context is null), the context-sensitive production behaves as a simple substitution for a single variable. When the context does not match, no substitution can be made.

The use of the word *context* above refers to the production rules of a grammar, so care should be taken not to confuse this meaning with the more general use to describe phrases in sentences. When trying to find a production sequence that generates a given sentence generated by a context-free grammar, we may well have to consider the context in which phrases of the sentence appear.

Context-free grammars generate a large and rich class of languages; and they, or subsets of them, will be the subject of the rest of this chapter and succeeding chapters. From now on, unless stated otherwise, the word *grammar* will imply context-free grammar.

Examples: Let $\Sigma = \{A, B, C\}$, $T = \{\alpha, \beta, \gamma\}$, and $G = (\Sigma, T, \Pi, \alpha)$.

(a) $$\Pi = \{\alpha \rightarrow \beta \qquad :1$$
$$\beta \rightarrow AB\alpha \qquad :2\}$$

G is context-free.

(b) $$\Pi = \{ \alpha \rightarrow \alpha\beta \qquad :1$$
$$\alpha\beta \rightarrow \alpha\gamma \qquad :2$$
$$\gamma \rightarrow AB\alpha \qquad :3\}$$

G is context-sensitive.

(c) $$\Pi = \{ \alpha \rightarrow \alpha\beta \qquad :1$$
$$\alpha\beta \rightarrow \beta\gamma \qquad :2$$
$$\beta \rightarrow A \qquad :3\}$$

G is neither context-free nor context-sensitive, although it is a phrase-structure grammar.

As a more elaborate example of a context-free grammar, let us define one that generates a language more like a programming language. The language defined will be the set of arithmetic expressions composed of the additive, multiplicative, and exponential operators. In this simple grammar the operands will be designated by single letters of the alphabet. Let

$$G_A = (\Sigma, T, \Pi, \sigma)$$

where

$$\Sigma = \{A, B, C, \ldots, Z\} \cup \{(,), \times, /, +, -, \uparrow\}$$

T = {⟨*arithmetic expression*⟩, ⟨*multiplying operator*⟩, ⟨*term*⟩,
   ⟨*adding operator*⟩, ⟨*primary*⟩, ⟨*factor*⟩, ⟨*operand*⟩}

σ = ⟨*arithmetic expression*⟩

Π = {⟨*adding operator*⟩ → +	: 1
⟨*adding operator*⟩ → −	: 2
⟨*multiplying operator*⟩ → ×	: 3
⟨*multiplying operator*⟩ → /	: 4
⟨*primary*⟩ → ⟨*operand*⟩	: 5
⟨*primary*⟩ → (⟨*arithmetic expression*⟩)	: 6
⟨*factor*⟩ → ⟨*primary*⟩	: 7
⟨*factor*⟩ → ⟨*factor*⟩ ↑ ⟨*primary*⟩	: 8
⟨*term*⟩ → ⟨*factor*⟩	: 9
⟨*term*⟩ → ⟨*term*⟩ ⟨*multiplying operator*⟩ ⟨*factor*⟩	:10
⟨*arithmetic expression*⟩ → ⟨*term*⟩	:11
⟨*arithmetic expression*⟩ → ⟨*adding operator*⟩ ⟨*term*⟩	:12
⟨*arithmetic expression*⟩ → ⟨*arithmetic expression*⟩	
⟨*adding operator*⟩ ⟨*term*⟩	:13
⟨*operand*⟩ → A	:14

⟨*operand*⟩ → Z   :40}

Thus Λ(G) is the set of all strings of symbols in Σ ($\bar{x} \in \Sigma$*) such that

$$\langle arithmetic\ expression \rangle \overset{*}{\Rightarrow} \bar{x}$$

As a final example, let us show that the expression (A + B) is in Λ(G).

⟨*arithmetic expression*⟩ $\overset{11}{\Rightarrow}$ ⟨*term*⟩
$\overset{9}{\Rightarrow}$ ⟨*factor*⟩
$\overset{7}{\Rightarrow}$ ⟨*primary*⟩
$\overset{6}{\Rightarrow}$ (⟨*arithmetic expression*⟩)
$\overset{13}{\Rightarrow}$ (⟨*arithmetic expression*⟩ ⟨*adding operator*⟩ ⟨*term*⟩)
$\overset{11}{\Rightarrow}$ (⟨*term*⟩ ⟨*adding operator*⟩ ⟨*term*⟩)
$\overset{9}{\Rightarrow}$ (⟨*factor*⟩ ⟨*adding operator*⟩ ⟨*term*⟩)
$\overset{7}{\Rightarrow}$ (⟨*primary*⟩ ⟨*adding operator*⟩ ⟨*term*⟩)
$\overset{5}{\Rightarrow}$ (⟨*operand*⟩ ⟨*adding operator*⟩ ⟨*term*⟩)
$\overset{14}{\Rightarrow}$ (A ⟨*adding operator*⟩ ⟨*term*⟩)
$\overset{1}{\Rightarrow}$ (A + ⟨*term*⟩)
$\overset{9}{\Rightarrow}$ (A + ⟨*factor*⟩)
$\overset{7}{\Rightarrow}$ (A + ⟨*primary*⟩)
$\overset{5}{\Rightarrow}$ (A + ⟨*operand*⟩)
$\overset{15}{\Rightarrow}$ (A + B)

problems

1. Suppose

$$\Pi = \{\sigma \to A\xi \quad : 1$$
$$\xi \to \alpha \quad : 2$$
$$\xi \to B \quad : 3$$
$$\alpha \to C \quad : 4\}$$

Indicate whether the following statements are true or false.

(a) $\sigma \Rightarrow A$

(b) $\sigma \overset{*}{\Rightarrow} A$

(c) $\xi \overset{*}{\Rightarrow} \alpha C$

(d) $A\sigma \overset{*}{\Rightarrow} AAB$

(e) $A\xi B \overset{*}{\Rightarrow} ACB$

2. Use the following productions as substitution rules and show that, for any positive integer n,

$$\langle positive\ integer\rangle \overset{*}{\Rightarrow} n$$

The substitution rules are:

$\langle positive\ integer\rangle \to \langle leading\ digit\rangle$
$\langle positive\ integer\rangle \to \langle positive\ integer\rangle\ \langle digit\rangle$
$\langle leading\ digit\rangle \to 1$
$\langle leading\ digit\rangle \to 2$
. . . .
$\langle leading\ digit\rangle \to 9$
$\langle digit\rangle \to \langle leading\ digit\rangle$
$\langle digit\rangle \to 0$

Note that the second production in the above set has a variable, *⟨positive integer⟩*, which appears on both left- and right-hand sides. The string substituted for the variable contains the same variable again. This technique is very powerful, and we will see it used often. Such a production is called *recursive*.

3. Given the following productions

$\langle statement\ label\rangle \to \langle letter\rangle\ \langle four\text{-}digit\ number\rangle$
$\langle letter\rangle \to A$
$\langle letter\rangle \to B$
$\langle four\text{-}digit\ number\rangle \to 1001$
$\langle four\text{-}digit\ number\rangle \to 1002$

(*a*) Construct a sequence of substitutions whereby

$$\langle statement\ label \rangle \overset{*}{\Rightarrow} A1001$$

(*b*) Construct a different sequence for the same production.

4. Let
$$G_0 = (\{A\}, \{\alpha\}, \Pi, \alpha)$$
where
$$\Pi = \{\alpha \rightarrow A \qquad :1$$
$$\alpha \rightarrow A\alpha A \qquad :2\}$$

Show that $\Lambda(G_0) = A^{2n-1}$, for $n = 1, 2, \ldots$

5. Complete the demonstration that G_G (see Section 3.4) is a generating grammar for

$$f(n) = \sum_{i=1}^{n} i$$

6. Construct the generating grammar for

$$f(n) = n^2$$

7. Are the following phrase-structure grammars? If so, characterize them as context-free or context-sensitive.

$$G = (\{A, B\}, \{\alpha, \beta\}, \Pi, \alpha)$$

(*a*) $\Pi = \{\alpha \rightarrow \varepsilon \qquad :1$
$\qquad \alpha \rightarrow \beta \qquad :2$
$\qquad \beta\alpha \rightarrow A \qquad :3$
$\qquad \varepsilon \rightarrow B \qquad :4\}$

(*b*) $\Pi = \{A \rightarrow \alpha \qquad :1$
$\qquad \alpha \rightarrow \beta \qquad :2$
$\qquad \beta \rightarrow A \qquad :3\}$

(*c*) $\Pi = \{\alpha \rightarrow A \qquad :1$
$\qquad \alpha \rightarrow \beta \qquad :2$
$\qquad \beta \rightarrow B \qquad :3\}$

8. Construct phrase-structure grammars to generate the following languages

(*a*) $\Lambda = \{A^{3n} \mid n \geq 1\}$

(*b*) $\Lambda = \{A^n B^{2m-1} \mid n, m \geq 1\}$

(*c*) $\Lambda = \{A^n B^n \mid n \geq 1\}$

(*d*) $\Lambda = \{A^n B^n C^n \mid n \geq 1\}$

9. Use the definition of arithmetic expressions above to find the production chain for the following arithmetic expressions.

    (a) A × (B + C ↑ D)

    (b) A × B × C ↑ D

10. Find a grammar that has as its language the set of all integers (positive, negative, and zero).

11. In production 13 of the arithmetic-expression grammar G_A, the variable ⟨*arithmetic expression*⟩ is repeated as the left-hand term of the right-hand side. This production is called *left recursive*. Left recursion causes problems with several translating schemes. Rewrite the grammar to produce the same language with no left-recursive productions.

4

properties of formal grammars

An extensive theory of context-free languages has been developed, and it is growing larger every day. It is not the purpose of this book to attempt a thorough presentation of the subject; however, some properties of context-free grammars (CFG) that are particularly useful in developing translation algorithms will be discussed in this chapter. Since nearly all of these algorithms deal with context-free grammars, the word grammar will, in the rest of the book, mean context-free unless otherwise stated.

4.1   *localized structure*

Context-free grammars show a localizing behavior that is useful in studying their structure and vital for translation algorithms involving them. By "localizing behavior" we mean that results of substitutions occurring in a region of the string remain in that region. Let us formalize this idea.

Lemma 4.1:   Let G be a grammar, and let $\bar{x}$ and $\bar{y}$ be two sentential forms produced by the grammar, such that

$$\bar{x} \Rightarrow \bar{y}$$

If $\bar{x}$ can be partitioned into two contiguous strings $\bar{x}_1$ and $\bar{x}_2$,

$$\bar{x} \Rightarrow \bar{x}_1\bar{x}_2$$

then there exists a partition of $\bar{y}$ into two substrings $\bar{y}_1$ and $\bar{y}_2$,

$$\bar{y} = \bar{y}_1\bar{y}_2$$

such that either

$$\bar{x}_1 \Rightarrow \bar{y}_1 \quad \text{and} \quad \bar{x}_2 = \bar{y}_2$$

or $\qquad\qquad\quad \bar{x}_1 = \bar{y}_1 \quad \text{and} \quad \bar{x}_2 \Rightarrow \bar{y}_2$

Proof: If

$$\bar{x}_1\bar{x}_2 \Rightarrow \bar{y}$$

there is a variable ξ in $\bar{y}$ and a production $\xi \to \bar{v}$ in Π that is applied to an occurrence of ξ in $\bar{x}$. Assume that the root ξ occurs in $\bar{x}_1$. (If not, it must occur in $\bar{x}_2$ and the proof is identical in structure.) Then

$$\bar{x}_1 = \bar{u}_1\xi\bar{u}_2$$

Then, after application of the production

$$\bar{y}_1 = \bar{u}_1\bar{v}\bar{u}_2$$

and $\qquad\qquad\qquad \bar{y}_2 = \bar{x}_2$

the result is

$$\bar{x}_1 \Rightarrow \bar{y}_1$$

and $\qquad\qquad\qquad \bar{x}_2 = \bar{y}_2$

A similar proof for ξ in $\bar{x}_2$ results in the conclusion that $\bar{x}_1 = \bar{y}_1$ and $\bar{x}_2 \Rightarrow \bar{y}_2$. Since $\bar{x} \overset{*}{\Rightarrow} \bar{y}$ means that there is a sequence of k (k $\geq$ 0) direct productions, the previous lemma can be applied k times to prove the following theorem.

Theorem 4.1: Let G be a grammar, and let $\bar{x}$ and $\bar{y}$ be two sentential forms generated by G such that

$$\bar{x} \overset{*}{\Rightarrow} \bar{y}$$

Then if

$$\bar{x} = \bar{x}_1\bar{x}_2$$

there exists a $\bar{y}_1$ and $\bar{y}_2$ such that

$$\bar{x}_1 \overset{*}{\Rightarrow} \bar{y}_1$$

and $\qquad\qquad\qquad \bar{x}_2 \overset{*}{\Rightarrow} \bar{y}_2$

Theorem 4.1 can be applied repeatedly to obtain the following more general form.

Theorem 4.2:   As in Theorem 4.1, let $\bar{x}$ and $\bar{y}$ be two sentential forms such that

$$\bar{x} \overset{*}{\Rightarrow} \bar{y}$$

Now let

$$\bar{x} = \bar{x}_1 \bar{x}_2 \cdots \bar{x}_n$$

Then there exist $\bar{y}_1, \bar{y}_2, \ldots, \bar{y}_n$ such that

$$\bar{y} = \bar{y}_1 \bar{y}_2 \cdots \bar{y}_n$$

and such that

$$\bar{x}_1 \overset{*}{\Rightarrow} \bar{y}_1$$
$$\bar{x}_2 \overset{*}{\Rightarrow} \bar{y}_2$$
$$\cdot$$
$$\cdot$$
$$\cdot$$
$$\bar{x}_n \overset{*}{\Rightarrow} \bar{y}_n$$

Figure 4.1 illustrates Theorem 4.2.   Suppose there is a sentential form

$$\bar{x} = \bar{x}_1 \bar{x}_2 \bar{x}_3$$

Let $\bar{y}$ be a sentential form star-produced by $\bar{x}$.

$$\bar{x} \overset{*}{\Rightarrow} \bar{y}$$

Then there is a partitioning of $\bar{y}$

$$\bar{y} = \bar{y}_1 \bar{y}_2 \bar{y}_3$$

such that the overall production is partitioned into a set of those parallel production sequences.

This property is one reason why context-free grammars are so useful as models since it allows sentence construction or analysis to be

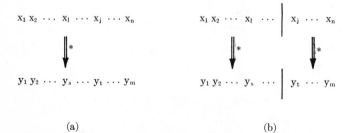

(a)   (b)

Figure 4.1 Partition of a star production into local sub-productions

split into subparts independent of one another. To see that this localized property is not a property of non-context-free languages, let us look at the following grammar, G_N.

$$G_N = (\Sigma, T, \Pi, \sigma)$$

for which the following productions are included in Π.

$$
\begin{array}{ll}
\sigma \to \mu\alpha & :1 \\
\alpha \to \alpha\alpha & :2 \\
\mu\alpha \to \alpha\mu & :3
\end{array}
$$

The strings $\bar{x} = \mu\alpha\alpha\alpha\alpha$ and $\bar{y} = \alpha\alpha\alpha\mu$ are sentential forms in G_N, and

$$\bar{x} \overset{*}{\Rightarrow} \bar{y}$$

by repeated application of production 3. Clearly, these strings violate the partitioning theorem for context-free grammars. Production 3, which is not context-free, allows the symbol μ to roam through the string, away from the region in which it originally appeared and across any partition boundaries that might be erected.

4.2   use of the localizing property

Now let us see how the theorems in Section 4.1 can be used to help analyze the character of languages generated by grammars. Let

$$G_E = (\{A, B\}, \{\sigma, \alpha, \beta\}, \Pi_E, \sigma)$$

where

$$
\begin{array}{ll}
\Pi_E = \{\sigma \to A\beta & :1 \\
\sigma \to B\alpha & :2 \\
\alpha \to A & :3 \\
\alpha \to A\sigma & :4 \\
\alpha \to B\alpha\alpha & :5 \\
\beta \to B & :6 \\
\beta \to B\sigma & :7 \\
\beta \to A\beta\beta & :8\}
\end{array}
$$

Now, for any symbol a, the number of a's in a string $\bar{x}$ is designated by the notation $|\bar{x}|_a$. The language $\Lambda(G_E)$ consists of all strings of length with equal numbers (at least one) of A's and B's in any sequence. In the formal notation,

$$\Lambda(G) = \{\bar{x} \mid |\bar{x}|_A = |\bar{x}|_B \geq 1\} \tag{4.1}$$

Induction will be used to prove the preceding statement. The following three inductive hypotheses will be proved together.

$$|\bar{x}|_A = |\bar{x}|_B \qquad \text{iff } \sigma \overset{*}{\Rightarrow} \bar{x}, \ |\bar{x}| \le n \qquad (4.2)$$

$$|\bar{x}|_A = |\bar{x}|_B + 1 \qquad \text{iff } \alpha \overset{*}{\Rightarrow} \bar{x}, \ |\bar{x}| \le n - 1 \qquad (4.3)$$

$$|\bar{x}|_A + 1 = |\bar{x}_B| \qquad \text{iff } \beta \overset{*}{\Rightarrow} \bar{x}, \ |\bar{x}| \le n - 1 \qquad (4.4)$$

Hypothesis (4.2) is, of course, the statement of (4.1) if it can be shown to hold for all n. The hypotheses are clearly true for n = 2. Assume they are true for one value of n > 2. Start with Hypothesis (4.3). Suppose

$$\alpha \overset{*}{\Rightarrow} \bar{x} \qquad \text{and} \qquad |\bar{x}| = n$$

Then either

$$\alpha \Rightarrow A\sigma \Rightarrow \cdots \Rightarrow \bar{x}$$

or

$$\alpha \Rightarrow B\alpha\alpha \Rightarrow \cdots \Rightarrow \bar{x}$$

Thus either

$$A\sigma \overset{*}{\Rightarrow} \bar{x} \qquad \text{or} \qquad B\alpha\alpha \overset{*}{\Rightarrow} \bar{x}$$

Assume, first, that $A\sigma \overset{*}{\Rightarrow} \bar{x}$. Then applying Theorem 4.1 yields $\bar{x} = A\bar{y}$, where

$$\sigma \overset{*}{\Rightarrow} \bar{y}$$

Now $|\bar{y}| = m - 1$ and, by the inductive hypothesis,

$$|\bar{y}|_A = |\bar{y}|_B$$

thus

$$|\bar{x}|_A = |\bar{y}|_A + 1 = |\bar{y}|_B + 1 = |\bar{x}|_B + 1$$

Assume now that

$$B\alpha\alpha \overset{*}{\Rightarrow} \bar{x}$$

Then, by Theorem 4.2,

$$\bar{x} = By_1y_2$$

where

$$\alpha \overset{*}{\Rightarrow} \bar{y}_1 \qquad \text{and} \qquad \alpha \overset{*}{\Rightarrow} \bar{y}_2$$

Now

$$|\bar{x}|_B = 1 + |\bar{y}_1|_B + |\bar{y}_2|_B$$

By hypothesis, since $|\bar{y}_1|$ and $|\bar{y}_2| \le n - 1$,

$$|\bar{y}_1|_A = |\bar{y}_1|_B + 1$$

and

$$|\bar{y}_2|_A = |\bar{y}_2|_B + 1$$

so

$$|\bar{x}|_B = |\bar{y}_1|_A + |\bar{y}_2|_A - 1$$

and thus

$$|\bar{x}|_B + 1 = |\bar{y}_1|_A + |\bar{y}_2|_A = |\bar{x}|_A$$

In a similar manner, it can be shown that if

$$\beta \overset{*}{\Rightarrow} |\bar{x}| \qquad \text{and} \qquad |\bar{x}| = n$$

then

$$|\bar{x}|_A + 1 = |\bar{x}|_B$$

Now assume that

$$\sigma \overset{*}{\Rightarrow} \bar{x} \qquad \text{and} \qquad |\bar{x}| = n + 1$$

Then either

$$\sigma = A\beta \Rightarrow \cdots \Rightarrow \bar{x}$$

or

$$\sigma = B\alpha \Rightarrow \cdots \Rightarrow \bar{x}$$

Suppose the first chain occurs. By using the same arguments as above,

$$\bar{x} = A\bar{y} \qquad \text{and} \qquad \beta \overset{*}{\Rightarrow} \bar{y}$$

Since $|\bar{y}| = n$,

$$|\bar{y}|_A + 1 = |\bar{y}|_B$$

Thus

$$|\bar{x}|_A = |\bar{y}|_A + 1 = |\bar{y}|_B = |\bar{x}|_B$$

The second chain leads to the same conclusion through similar steps. Thus

$$|\bar{x}|_A = |\bar{x}|_B \qquad \text{for} \qquad |\bar{x}| \le m + 1$$

4.3   independence of production order; canonical form

Theorem 4.1 also implies the following result.

Theorem 4.3:   Let $\bar{x} \overset{*}{\Rightarrow} \bar{y}$ be the sequence of productions

$$p_1, p_2, \ldots, p_i, p_{i+1}, \ldots, p_n$$

Suppose that we can partition $\bar{x} = \bar{x}_1\bar{x}_2$ and $\bar{y} = \bar{y}_1\bar{y}_2$ such that p_i occurs in the production chain for $\bar{x}_1 \overset{*}{\Rightarrow} \bar{y}_1$ and p_{i+1} occurs in the production chain for $\bar{x}_2 \overset{*}{\Rightarrow} \bar{y}_2$. Then $\bar{x} \overset{*}{\Rightarrow} \bar{y}$ also by the sequence of productions

$$p_1, p_2, \ldots, p_{i-1}, p_{i+1}, p_i, p_{i+2}, \ldots, p_n$$

That is, according to Theorem 4.3 the order of substitutions can be reversed with no effect on the final result. The sequence is effectively the same production chain. The problem is that we are choosing to represent a two-dimensional structure, a tree, in a one-dimensional string. However, there are many such one-dimensional representations.

As an example, take the string

$$A\xi B\nu C$$

and the productions

$$\xi \rightarrow B \quad :1$$
$$\nu \rightarrow B \quad :2$$

There are the two sequences possible:

$$A\xi B\nu C \overset{1}{\Rightarrow} ABB\nu C \overset{2}{\Rightarrow} ABBBC$$
$$A\xi B\nu C \overset{2}{\Rightarrow} A\xi BBC \overset{1}{\Rightarrow} ABBBC$$

Another way of looking at it is that the two substitutions can take place in parallel since they are mutually independent. This operation is illustrated in Figure 4.2.

Since there are usually many possible one-dimensional representations of a partially ordered set, a single representative form called the *canonical production sequence* is defined.

Definition 4.1: Let $\bar{z}_1 \overset{*}{\Rightarrow} \bar{z}_n$. Then the sequence

$$\bar{z}_1 \overset{p_1}{\Rightarrow} \bar{z}_2 \overset{p_2}{\Rightarrow} \ldots \overset{p_3}{\Rightarrow} \bar{z}_n$$

is called a *canonical production sequence* if and only if each production is applied to the leftmost variable remaining in the string.

The canonical form of any production sequence $p_1, p_2, \ldots, p_n$ for $\bar{x} \overset{*}{\Rightarrow} \bar{y}$ can be generated by applying the following rule as many times as necessary.

Let $\bar{x} = \bar{x}_1\bar{x}_2$. If p_i is in the sequence for $\bar{x}_2 \overset{*}{\Rightarrow} \bar{y}_2$ while p_{i+1} is in that for $\bar{x}_1 \overset{*}{\Rightarrow} \bar{y}_1$, then interchange p_i and p_{i+1}. By Theorem 4.3, the new sequence formed is also one for $\bar{x} \overset{*}{\Rightarrow} \bar{y}$.

Suppose that after a finite number of interchanges there is a sequence $p_1, p_2, \ldots, p_n$ in which no further interchanges are possible. Then the chain is canonical. This is clearly so since either each p_{i+1} is applied to a substring of $\bar{x}$ to the right of the substring to which p_i is applied, or p_{i+1} is applied to a variable in the argument of p_i.

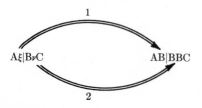

Figure 4.2 Parallel productions

It is also simple to show that the sequence of steps must terminate. To do this, a nonnegative number is associated with each chain. This number, which must decrease each time a transposition is performed, is

$$N = \sum_{i=1}^{n} f_i$$

where f_i is the number of productions to the right of p_i such that they operate independently on variables in substrings to the left of the phrase generated by p_i. Some number f_i must decrease by 1 each time a transposition is performed, so the sequence must be finite.

There is no guarantee, of course, that there is only one canonical form of the production sequence. If there is a sentence with more than one canonical production sequence from the starting variable, the grammar is called *ambiguous*. Production sequences arise from the grammar, and thus ambiguity is an inherent property of the grammar. However, there are many possible grammars that can produce a given language, and not all the grammars are necessarily ambiguous. A language may be generated by both ambiguous and unambiguous grammars.

For example, the grammar with the production set

$$\Pi = \{\sigma \to \alpha B \quad :1$$
$$\sigma \to A\beta \quad :2$$
$$\alpha \to A \quad :3$$
$$\beta \to B \quad :4\}$$

has as its language the single string AB. But there are two canonical production chains for that string:

$$\sigma \Rightarrow \alpha B \Rightarrow AB$$

and
$$\sigma \Rightarrow A\beta \Rightarrow AB$$

Thus G is an ambiguous grammar. But a grammar with the production set

$$\Pi = \{\sigma \to \alpha B \quad :1$$
$$\alpha \to A \quad :2\}$$

produces the same language unambiguously.

4.4   graphical representation of production chains

We mentioned that a production sequence is inherently a two-dimensional process since substitutions in different parts of a string are independent and thus can be considered to occur simultaneously. In mathematical terms, to write a production sequence is to impose an artificial total ordering on a set that is only partially ordered. This process causes a multiplicity of representations for a single sequence and requires the definition of a canonical production sequence.

There is a representation for production sequences that is much more satisfying intuitively, that provides only one form for each unique production sequence, and that will be used throughout the rest of the book when discussing sentence production and analysis. Let

$$\xi \rightarrow u_1 u_2 \cdot \cdot \cdot u_n$$

be a production in a grammar. The graphical representation of that production is shown in Figure 4.3(a). That is, the graphical representation of the production has, as its root (or parent) node, the left-hand side or root of the production. The descendant nodes from left to right are the symbols in the right-hand-side string in the same order.

The graph of a production sequence is assembled by attaching to each node representing a variable the production in the sequence that operates on that variable. In the above example where the production set was

$$\Pi = \{\sigma \rightarrow \alpha B \quad :1$$
$$\alpha \rightarrow B \quad :2\}$$

the string AB had the following production chain:

$$\sigma \overset{1}{\Rightarrow} \alpha B \overset{2}{\Rightarrow} AB$$

The graph of this chain appears in Figure 4.3(b).

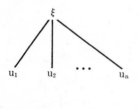

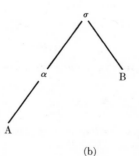

(a)   (b)

Figure 4.3 Graphs of productions

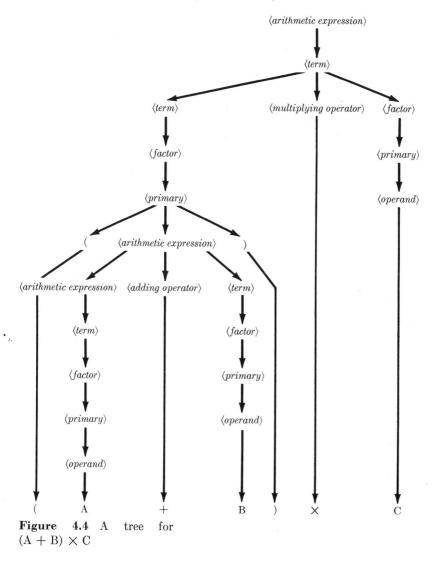

Figure   4.4   A   tree   for
$(A + B) \times C$

A more complex example would be the tree representing the chain producing the sentence

$$(A + B) \times C$$

generated by the grammar G_A given at the end of Chapter 3. This tree is shown in Figure 4.4. Another example of a tree, this one corresponding to an English sentence, is shown in Figure 4.5.

Ambiguity is defined as a sentence that has more than one distinct production tree. To illustrate, consider a classic example of an

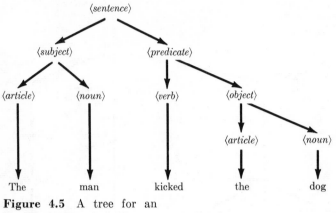

Figure 4.5 A tree for an
English sentence

ambiguous sentence, **They are flying planes.** Is **flying** an adjective
modifying **planes** or is it a verb? This ambiguity is structurally
represented in Figure 4.6.

4.5   binary translation trees

There is another graphical structure for a production tree that, although not as intuitively satisfying at first, will be very useful later.
The structure involves forming a binary tree from the general production tree. There is a procedure for forming the binary equivalent of
a general tree.   If T is a general tree, the binary equivalent tree B(T)
is constructed by applying the following two rules to all pairs of nodes
in the tree.   Let a and b be two nodes in T.

Rule 1:   The node b is the left descendant of a in B(T) if and only
if b is the leftmost descendant of a in T.

Rule 2:   The node b is the right descendant of a in B(T) if and only
if b is the next rightmost sibling of a in T.

For example, the tree in Figure 4.7(a) is a general tree, and its
binary equivalent tree is shown in Figure 4.7(b). The tree for the
sentence **The man kicked the dog,** shown earlier, would have as its
binary equivalent the tree in Figure 4.8. The binary-equivalent tree
for the arithmetic-expression derivation shown previously in this section appears in Figure 4.9.

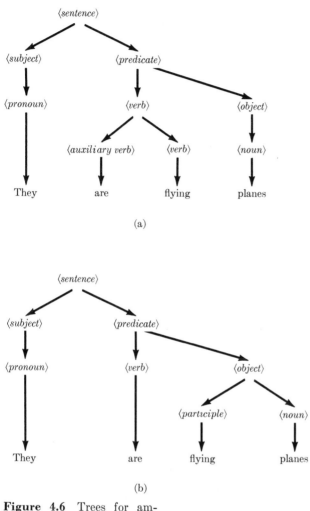

(a)

(b)

Figure 4.6 Trees for ambiguous sentence

At first glance this representation appears much less satisfying than a general tree. The terminal symbols in a general production tree are all dangling at the ends of the branches, and it is possible to distort the tree slightly so that the sentence produced appears at the bottom in proper order. The terminal symbols in a binary tree are distributed through the tree and no distortion can display the sentence. Furthermore, in a general tree all variable symbols

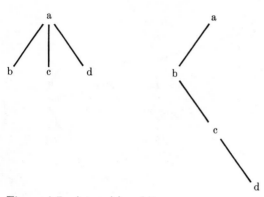

Figure 4.7   A tree (a) and its
binary equivalent (b)

are intermediate nodes with descendants, and all terminal symbols
have no descendants; that is, they are also terminal nodes of the tree.
However, the binary representation has some advantages that will
become clearer as it is used.

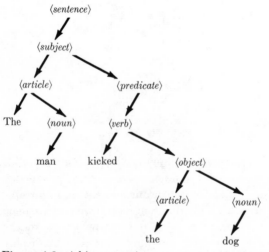

Figure 4.8   A binary-equivalent tree for an English
sentence

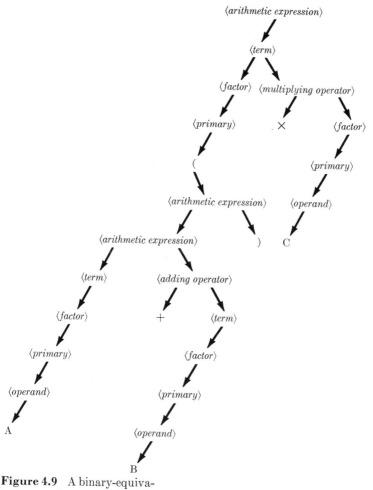

Figure 4.9   A binary-equivalent tree for an arithmetic
expression

4.6   *properties of binary translation trees*

These advantages depend on some structural properties that will be
discussed now.   First, however, let us define some elements of binary
production trees.

A *left-hand chain* (or *right-hand chain*) of a binary tree is a sequence of
nodes $a_1, a_2, \ldots, a_n$ $(n \geq 1)$ where a_i is the left (right) descendant of a_{i-1}, for $i = 2, \ldots, n$.

A chain, $a_1, \ldots, a_n$ is *contained* in a chain $b_1, b_2, \ldots, b_m$ iff there exists a $j \geq 0$ such that $a_i = b_{j+i}$, for $i = 1, 2, \ldots, n$ ($n \leq m$). The chain $a_1, a_2, \ldots, a_n$ is then a *subchain* of chain $b_1, b_2, \ldots, b_m$.

A chain is a *maximal chain* iff it is contained in no other chain than itself.

Figure 4.10(a), shows a binary tree T. Figure 4.10(b) shows some left- and right-hand chains in T, and (c) shows some maximal left- and right-hand chains.

In the following statements, T is again a general translation tree and B(T) is its binary equivalent. Left-hand chains can be defined for general trees in the same way they are defined for binary trees. The following lemmas follow directly from the definition of the transformation.

Lemma 4.2:   Left-hand chains in B(T) are left-hand chains in T and vice versa.

Since siblings descended from a node in T are terms in the right-hand side of some production, the following lemma is true.

Lemma 4.3:   A maximal right-hand chain in B(T) is the argument of a production p. The parent of the first node in the chain is the root of p.

Since any variable node in T must have at least one descendant, we have the following lemma about maximal left-hand chains.

Lemma 4.4:   A maximal left-hand chain in B(T) contains only one terminal symbol, and that is the last node in the chain.

4.7   *phrases*

Phrases in sentential forms are substrings derived from single variables in a production sequence. Since the variable from which a phrase is derived is not necessarily the starting variable, phrases themselves are not necessarily sentential forms, but they are analogous.

Definition 4.2:   Let $\bar{x}$ be a sentential form in a language $\Lambda(G)$, and let $\bar{x}$ be partitioned into three substrings as follows

$$\bar{x} = \bar{x}_1 \bar{x}_2 \bar{x}_3$$

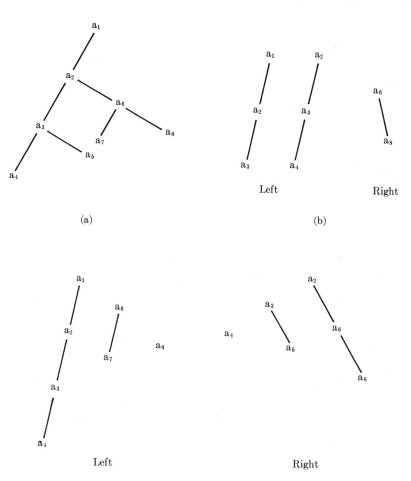

Figure 4.10 Chains in binary trees: (a) binary tree; (b) left- and right-hand chains of (a); (c) maximal left- and right-hand chains of (a)

Now $\bar{x}_2$ is a *phrase* of $\bar{x}$ if and only if there is a production sequence for $\bar{x}$ containing a string $\bar{y}$ of the form

$$\bar{y} = \bar{x}_1 \xi \bar{x}_2$$

where

$$\sigma \overset{*}{\Rightarrow} \bar{y} \overset{*}{\Rightarrow} \bar{x}$$

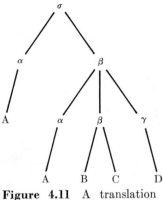

Figure 4.11 A translation tree for AABCD

In terms of the graphical representation, $\bar{x}_2$ is a phrase if and only if it is a string of symbols descended from a single node ξ. In the translation tree in Figure 4.11, for example, ABCD is a phrase, as are BC and $\alpha\beta\gamma$.

A phrase that contains no other phrases is called a *prime phrase*. Above, A and BC are examples of prime phrases. The *handle* of a sentence is the leftmost prime phrase in it. The handle of the sentence AABCD above is the first A.

4.8 ε-free languages

Often it is desired to modify grammars that produce certain languages in order to obtain a grammar that produces the same language, but has different properties that make translation easier. When making modifications, care must be taken to retain the complexity necessary for the semantic interpretation to remain the same.

One modification often made is to remove productions with the empty string on the right-hand side. Such a modified grammar is called, naturally enough, an ε-*free grammar*. Given a grammar $G = (\Sigma, T, \Pi, \sigma)$, the following algorithm will produce a modified grammar G' which is ε-free.

Step 1: Let $\Pi_1 = \{\xi \to \bar{u} \mid \text{for all } \xi \to \bar{u} \in \Pi, \bar{u} \neq \varepsilon\}$.

That is, let Π_1 be the set of all productions not having ε as their argument.

Step 2:   Let $\Phi = \{\xi \mid \xi \overset{*}{\Rightarrow} \varepsilon \text{ in } G\}$.

Φ is the set of all variables that could star-produce ε in G.

Step 3: Π_2 is formed from Π in the following manner.   For each production

$$\xi \rightarrow \bar{u} \in \Pi$$

if

$$\bar{u} = \bar{u}_1 \nu \bar{u}_2$$

where $\bar{u}_1$ or $\bar{u}_2$ or both are non-null and $\nu \in \Phi$, then add $\xi \rightarrow \bar{u}_1 \bar{u}_2$ to Π_2.

Finally, the new production set Π' is formed from Π_1 and Π_2.

Step 4:   Let $\Pi' = \Pi_1 \cup \Pi_2$.

As a simple example, let

$$\Pi = \{\sigma \rightarrow A\xi B \qquad :1$$
$$\xi \rightarrow \varepsilon \qquad :2$$
$$\xi \rightarrow A \qquad :3\}$$

Then

$$\Pi_1 = \{\sigma \rightarrow A\xi B \qquad :1$$
$$\xi \rightarrow A \qquad :2\}$$
$$\Phi = \{\xi\}$$
$$\Pi_2 = \{\sigma \rightarrow AB\}$$

and

$$\Pi' = \{\sigma \rightarrow A\xi B \qquad :1$$
$$\sigma \rightarrow AB \qquad :2$$
$$\xi \rightarrow A \qquad :3\}$$

In this simple case, it should be clear that $\Lambda(G) = \Lambda(G')$.   With one minor modification this statement is true in general.   Consider the following production set of a grammar G:

$$\Pi = \{\sigma \rightarrow \xi \qquad :1$$
$$\xi \rightarrow A \qquad :2$$
$$\xi \rightarrow \varepsilon \qquad :3\}$$

and let Π' be the production set for the ε-free grammar G' constructed from G by using the algorithm

$$\Pi' = \{\sigma \rightarrow \xi \qquad :1$$
$$\xi \rightarrow A \qquad :2\}$$

Now,

$$\Lambda(G) = \{A, \varepsilon\}$$

but

$$\Lambda(G') = \{A\}$$

Step 3 could not be applied to production 1 in Π_1 because ξ must have a nonzero context; otherwise $\bar{u}_1\bar{u}_2$ in step 3 would be ε and a production $\xi \to \varepsilon$ would be introduced into Π_2. Thus the following theorem holds.

Theorem 4.4:   Let G be a grammar (Σ, T, Π, σ) and let G′ be an ε-free grammar constructed by the algorithm above.   Then

$$\Lambda(G') = \Lambda(G) - \{\varepsilon\}$$

Proof: First, assume that

$$\bar{x} \in \Lambda(G')$$

Then

$$\sigma \overset{*}{\Rightarrow} \bar{x}$$

by productions in Π', and

$$\sigma \overset{p_1'}{\Rightarrow} \bar{u}_1 \overset{p_2'}{\Rightarrow} u_2 \cdots \overset{p_n'}{\Rightarrow} \bar{x}$$

If all p_i' are in Π_1 (as defined in the algorithm), they are also in Π and

$$\sigma \overset{*}{\Rightarrow} \bar{x}$$

by productions in Π.   Now assume that a p_i' is in Π_2.   Let p_i' be

$$\xi \to \bar{z}$$

so that

$$\bar{u}_{i-1} = \bar{y}_1 \xi \bar{y}_2 \qquad \text{and} \qquad \bar{u}_i = \bar{y}_1 \bar{z} \bar{y}_2$$

According to the construction of Π_2, there is a production p_j in Π of the form

$$\xi \to \bar{z}_1 \nu \bar{z}_2$$

where

$$\bar{z} = \bar{z}_1 \bar{z}_2 \qquad \text{and} \qquad \nu \overset{*}{\Rightarrow} \varepsilon \text{ in G}$$

Thus, for the sequence in Π',

$$\bar{u}_{i-1} \overset{p_i'}{\Rightarrow} \bar{u}_i$$

we can substitute the production sequence in Π

$$\bar{u}_{i-1} = \bar{y}_1 \xi \bar{y}_2 \overset{p_j}{\Rightarrow} \bar{y}_1 \bar{z}_1 \nu \bar{z}_2 \bar{y}_2 \overset{*}{\Rightarrow} \bar{y}_1 \bar{z}_1 \bar{z}_2 \bar{y}_2 = \bar{y}_1 \bar{z} \bar{y}_2 = \bar{u}_i$$

So, if $\sigma \overset{*}{\Rightarrow} \bar{x}$ by a production sequence in Π', there is a production sequence in Π such that $\sigma \overset{*}{\Rightarrow} \bar{x}$.   So

$$\bar{x} \in \Lambda(G)$$

Now assume that

$$\bar{x} \in \Lambda(G) \qquad \text{and} \qquad \bar{x} \neq \varepsilon$$

Then

$$\sigma \xrightarrow{p_1} \bar{u}_1 \xrightarrow{p_2} \bar{u}_2 \cdots \xrightarrow{p_i} \bar{x}$$

If no productions are ε-producing, then they are all in Π_1, and thus in Π'. So $\sigma \xrightarrow{*} \bar{x}$ in Π'. Now assume that

$$\bar{u}_{i-1} \xrightarrow{p_i} \bar{u}_i$$

where p_i is a production of the form

$$\nu \rightarrow \varepsilon$$

so

$$\bar{u}_{i-1} = \bar{z}_1 \nu \bar{z}_2 \xrightarrow{p_i} \bar{z}_1 \bar{z}_2 = \bar{u}_i$$

Now the variable ν first appears somewhere earlier in the sequence. If it appears as the result of a chain of single variable substitutions

$$\xi_1 \rightarrow \xi_2, \ \xi_2 \rightarrow \xi_3, \ \ldots, \ \xi_m \rightarrow \nu$$

trace back to the first occurrence of the first variable in ξ_1 in the chain. Assume it is first generated in a nonzero context in the production step from u_j to u_{j+1}:

$$\bar{u}_j = \bar{\omega}_1 \bar{\omega}_1 \xrightarrow{p_{j+1}} \bar{\omega}_1 \bar{\omega}_3 \xi \bar{\omega}_4 \bar{\omega}_2$$

Since $\xi \xrightarrow{*} \varepsilon$, there is a production p'_{j+1} in Π' corresponding to p_{j+1}:

$$\mu \rightarrow \bar{\omega}_3 \bar{\omega}_4$$

So the production steps

$$\xi_1 \rightarrow \xi_2, \ \ldots, \ \xi_m \rightarrow \nu \qquad \text{and} \qquad \nu \rightarrow \varepsilon$$

are eliminated from the sequence and the production p'_{j+1} is substituted, generating the same sentential form $\bar{u}_i$.

Thus there is a sequence of productions, all in Π', which generates $\bar{x}$, and thus

$$\bar{x} \in \Lambda(G')$$

The concept behind this proof is not as complex as the proof is long, and working at more examples will convince the reader intuitively that this theorem is true.

problems

1. Prove Theorem 4.1.

2. Prove Theorem 4.2.

3. Identify the language generated by each of the following grammars and prove it is the correct language.

   (a) $G = (\{A, B\}, \{\sigma, \alpha, \beta\}, \Pi, \sigma)$
        $\Pi = \{\sigma \rightarrow A\alpha \quad :1$
        $\phantom{\Pi = \{}\alpha \rightarrow A \quad :2$
        $\phantom{\Pi = \{}\alpha \rightarrow \beta \quad :3$
        $\phantom{\Pi = \{}\beta \rightarrow B\beta \quad :4$
        $\phantom{\Pi = \{}\beta \rightarrow B \quad :5\}$

   (b) $G = (\{A, B\}, \{\sigma, \alpha, \beta\}, \Pi, \sigma)$
        $\Pi = \{\sigma \rightarrow A\beta A \quad :1$
        $\phantom{\Pi = \{}\alpha \rightarrow A\beta A \quad :2$
        $\phantom{\Pi = \{}\alpha \rightarrow A \quad :3$
        $\phantom{\Pi = \{}\beta \rightarrow B\alpha B \quad :4$
        $\phantom{\Pi = \{}\beta \rightarrow B \quad :5\}$

4. Show that, for any pair of phrases $\{\bar{x}_1, \bar{x}_2\}$ in a string $\bar{x}$, only one of the following three conditions holds:

   (a) $\bar{x}_1$ is totally contained in $\bar{x}_2$

   (b) $\bar{x}_2$ is totally contained in $\bar{x}_1$

   (c) $\bar{x}_1$ and $\bar{x}_2$ are disjoint

5. Do Theorems 4.1, 4.2, and 4.3 hold in general for context-sensitive languages? Show why or why not.

6. Use the grammar G_A for simple arithmetic expressions to show the canonical production sequences for the following sentences:

   (a) A

   (b) A + A

   (c) A × (A + A) + A

7. Are the following grammars ambiguous? Show why or why not.

   (a) $G = (\{A\}, \{\sigma, \alpha\}, \Pi, \sigma)$
        $\Pi = \{\sigma \rightarrow \alpha \quad :1$
        $\phantom{\Pi = \{}\alpha \rightarrow A\alpha A \quad :2$
        $\phantom{\Pi = \{}\alpha \rightarrow A \quad :3\}$

   (b) $G = (\{A, B, C\}, \{\sigma, \alpha, \beta\}, \Pi, \sigma)$
        $\Pi = \{\sigma \rightarrow \alpha\beta \quad :1$
        $\phantom{\Pi = \{}\alpha \rightarrow AB \quad :2$
        $\phantom{\Pi = \{}\alpha \rightarrow A \quad :3$
        $\phantom{\Pi = \{}\beta \rightarrow BC \quad :4$
        $\phantom{\Pi = \{}\beta \rightarrow C \quad :5\}$

8. For each of the following languages, construct both an ambiguous and an unambiguous grammar that generates it.

(a) $\Lambda(G) = \{A^n B^n \mid n \geq 2\}$

(b) $\Lambda(G) = \{(AB)^n \mid n \geq 2\}$

9. Use the arithmetic-expression grammar G_A once again, this time to construct translation trees for the three sentences in Problem 6.

10. Use the grammar G_E discussed in Section 4.3 to construct translation trees for the following strings:

(a) AAABBB

(b) AABABB

(c) ABABABBA

11. Do any of the sentences in Problem 10 have ambiguous production sequences? If so, show an alternative translation tree.

12. Construct the equivalent binary translation trees for the translation trees in Problem 9 and in Problem 10.

13. Show the left- and right-hand chains of the binary trees constructed in Problem 12.

14. Prove the following: (a) Lemma 4.2; (b) Lemma 4.3; and (c) Lemma 4.4.

15. Show all phrases, prime phrases, and handles of the following simple arithmetic expressions.

(a) $(A + A) \times A$

(b) $A + A + A + A$

(c) $A + A \times A + A \times (A)$

16. Discuss any connection you see between the syntactic phrases and the evaluation of an arithmetic expression.

17. Construct the ε-free grammar G' equivalent to the following grammars. In each case indicate whether $\Lambda(G') = \Lambda(G)$.

(a) $G = (\{A\}, \{\sigma, \alpha\}, \Pi, \sigma)$
$$\Pi = \{\sigma \to \alpha \qquad :1$$
$$\alpha \to A\alpha A \qquad :2$$
$$\alpha \to A \qquad :3$$
$$\alpha \to \varepsilon \qquad :4\}$$

(b) G $= (\{A, B, C\}, \{\sigma, \alpha, \beta, \gamma\}, \Pi, \sigma)$
   $\Pi = \{\sigma \rightarrow \alpha\beta$ $:1$
      $\alpha \rightarrow \gamma$ $:2$
      $\alpha \rightarrow AB$ $:3$
      $\gamma \rightarrow C$ $:4$
      $\beta \rightarrow A\alpha B$ $:5$
      $\gamma \rightarrow \varepsilon$ $:6\}$

5

structure of binary translation trees

It is finally time to discuss how sentences generated by context-free grammars are translated, or *parsed*. Given the grammar and the sentence of a computer language, for example, it is necessary to generate some representation of the translation tree used as a basis for the code generation. The first set of algorithms described are designed to operate on general context-free languages. Later, strong restrictions will be placed on the grammar to develop simpler and faster translators.

To simplify the algorithms, some simple restrictions will be placed on the grammars even now. These restrictions, however, will not limit the set of languages considered. On the other hand, the semantic content of a sentence is more deeply dependent on the specific grammar used to generate the sentence, and without a more precise mathematical theory of semantics than presented here, it is not possible to state as a theorem that the semantic content remains unchanged under these restrictions. But we can say that, for the most useful languages, the limitations required on the grammars (for instance, the ε-free restriction) do not appear to have a profound effect on the semantics of the language involved.

As you study the algorithms in the following chapters, you should always keep in mind the fact that there are as many algorithms as there are programmers and authors to generate them. Many factors can influence an algorithm design, not the least of which is style. Programming is still referred to by some, with justification, as an *art*. There are, however, more mundane but vital factors influencing the program design, such as the design of the computer used, the language used to program the algorithm, and the intended style of use for the translator.

The first parsing technique to be considered in this and the next chapter is called the *top-down parse*. There are many top-down parsing routines; some have been described in the literature. The algorithm discussed in Chapter 6 is particularly straightforward and simple. In addition, it will illuminate the basic concepts behind the top-down parse.

Suppose G is a grammar with the starting variable σ, and $\bar{s}$ is a sentence in the language generated by G. Then, before any processing, there is the following incomplete picture of the translation tree.

$$\sigma$$

$$S_1S_2S_3 \cdot \cdot \cdot S_n$$

Pretty incomplete, isn't it? Now the parsing algorithm uses the description of the grammar to fill in the picture. The simplest description of the top-down parse is that which motivates its name. The tree is filled in from top to bottom, albeit with a left-to-right bias.

Before we can consider the actual algorithm, though, it is necessary to look a little closer at the structure of translation trees. This structure is clearer if the binary form of the tree is used.

5.1 skeletons

Suppose that we have constructed a binary translation tree T from the starting variable σ to a sentence in the language $S_1S_2 \cdot \cdot \cdot S_n$.

Definition 5.1: The maximal left-hand chain from σ to S_1 is called the *backbone* of T.

If the tree in Figure 5.1(a) is a binary translation tree for $S_1S_2S_3$, then (b) shows the backbone of the tree, written $(\sigma, \alpha_1, \alpha_2, S_1)$ for compactness.

Let $(\sigma, \alpha_1, \alpha_2, \ldots, \alpha_m, S_1)$ be the backbone of a binary tree. Each node in the backbone is the left-hand element of a maximal right-hand chain that, according to Lemma 4.4, is, except for σ, the right-hand side of a production.

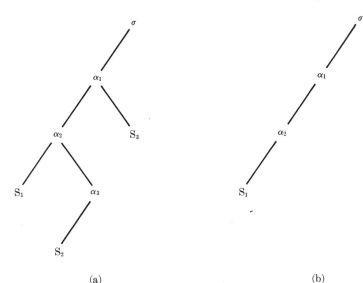

(a)   (b)

Figure   5.1   A   translation
tree (a) and its backbone (b)

Definition 5.2:   The backbone, along with the maximal right-hand
chains deriving from it, is called the *skeleton* of the production tree.

For example, suppose Figure 5.2 is the binary production tree
for $S_1 S_2 \cdots S_8$. Then the skeleton is shown in Figure 5.3. All
nodes in the tree are either in the skeleton or in subtrees left-descended
from variables in the right-hand chains. Thus producing the skeleton
will be the starting point for producing the full tree.

Given only σ and S_1, there are many possible skeletons, and only
a subset of these would usually be skeletons of legitimate translation
trees for the sentence. In fact, if the sentence is unambiguous, it
only has one production tree, and thus only one valid skeleton. The
possible skeletons must be tried one at a time until a valid translation
tree is found. To do this, it is convenient to *order* the skeletons
so the search can proceed in an orderly manner.

5.2   ordering skeletons

The, skeleton of a translation tree is shown schematically in Figure
5.4. Each branch represents a production of the form

$$\alpha_j \rightarrow \alpha_{j+1} b_1 b_2 \cdots b_k$$

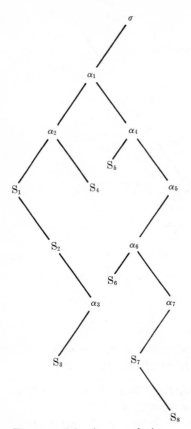

Figure 5.2 A translation
tree for $S_1S_2 \cdots S_8$

The productions are indexed, so there is a number associated with
each branch, the index of the production involved. The skeleton can
be represented uniquely by the finite ordered sequence

$$(i_1, i_2, \ldots , i_{n+1})$$

Definition 5.3: The sequence of production indices corresponding
to the right-hand chains from top to bottom in a skeleton is called
the *index of the skeleton.*

These skeleton indices can be ordered *lexicographically.* Lexicographic ordering is also known as *dictionary* ordering since it is
the technique used when putting words in alphabetical order. Assume
that we are given two sequences of numbers

$$R = (r_1, r_2, \ldots , r_n)$$

and
$$T = (t_1, t_2, \ldots , t_n)$$

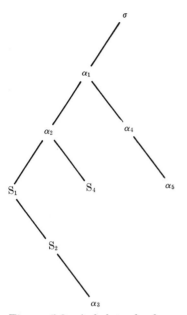

Figure 5.3   A skeleton backbone of translation tree in
Figure 5.2

and we wish to order R with respect to T, given that some ordering
of their individual elements already exists.   That is, there is some
order relationship between r_i and t_i, so that, for all i, either $r_i > t_i$,
$r_i = t_i$, or $r_i < t_i$.

The process of ordering them is as follows.   The first terms of
each sequence are examined.   If $r_1 > t_1$, then set $R > T$; if $r_1 < t_1$,
then set $R < T$.   However, if $r_1 = t_1$, move on and examine the
second terms, and so on through all of the terms if necessary.   For-
mally, $R \lessgtr T$ if and only if there is an $i \geq 1$ such that $r_i \lessgtr t_i$, and r_k
$= t_k$ for all $k < i$. $R = T$ if and only if $r_k = t_k$ for all $1 \leq k \leq n$.

Example: The two sets of sequences

(1, 3, 5, 9)	and	(a, a, b, e)
(2, 1, 0, 6)		(c, d, a, b)
(2, 1, 1, 13)		(c, d, b, a)
(5, 0, 20, 6)		(c, f, g, k)
(5, 0, 20, 20)		(r, a, a, a)
(A)		(B)

are in lexicographic order top to bottom, the first using numerical
order on the elements, the second using alphabetic order.

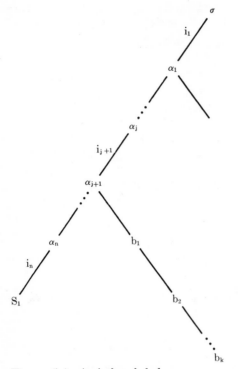

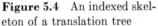

Figure 5.4   An indexed skeleton of a translation tree

The only possible problem with the procedure comes when comparing skeletons of different length.   How are they compared?   Luck-
ily, this is not really a problem because of the following property
that skeletons possess:

Remark 5.1:   Let $R = (r_1, r_2, \ldots, r_n)$ and $T = (t_1, t_2, \ldots, t_m)$ be
two indices of skeletons of a binary translation tree, where $m < n$.
Then R and T must differ within the first n terms, specifically $r_n \neq t_n$,
at least.

This observation is simple to prove since $r_n = S_1$, a terminal
symbol, and since t_n must be a variable symbol, by Lemma 4.4.   Thus
any two skeletons must differ in their first n terms, where n is the
length of the shorter of the two.

5.3   *generating skeletons*

The algorithm for constructing a left-hand chain from a given node
to a given terminal symbol is straightforward, the only complication

rising from the need to find the next candidate skeleton for the translation tree. To develop the algorithm, a particular set of data structures needs to be built from the production set of the grammar. In practice, the structures can be much more elaborate and the algorithms for using them correspondingly complex. This sophistication can either speed up the parsing or use less storage space. But it obscures the basic concept of the algorithm, so the simplest structure will be developed here.

The data needed for the skeleton generator are stored as a set of tables called *production tables*. There is a production table for each variable α, containing an entry for each production having α as its root. The information accessed is the index of the production and the initial leftmost term of the right-hand side. For example, let us suppose that in a grammar G, the productions having α on the left as root are

$$\alpha \rightarrow A \qquad :3$$
$$\alpha \rightarrow \gamma\alpha \qquad :7$$
$$\alpha \rightarrow B \qquad :9$$

Then the production table for α would be:

	Index	Term
1:	3	A
2:	7	γ
3:	9	B
4:	χ	χ

Entries of this table are referenced by the column name (*Index* or *Term*), as a function of the root α, and the row number. Since the number of rows differs for different variables, there is a special termination row with a special character designated by χ. Then, in the example above, we can designate particular information entries as

$$Index\ (\alpha,\ 2) = 7$$
$$Term\ (\alpha,\ 3) = B$$
$$Term\ (\alpha,\ 4) = \chi$$

The production tables are used in conjunction with another table, called a *connection matrix*, to construct the left-hand chain. This matrix can have many representations, but for our purposes it will be viewed as the result of a logical true-false function of two parameters. The matrix, or function, is referenced as follows

$$Connect(\alpha,\ b)$$

where α is a variable symbol and b is any symbol. The function has the value **True** if a left-hand chain of any length exists from the node α to the symbol b, and **False** if no such chain exists.

By using the production tables and the connection table, the following algorithm will produce a left-hand chain from a variable symbol to a terminal symbol. The procedure, called **Chain,** has as its parameters the set $(\alpha, S, LHC, Fail)$, where

$$\alpha = \text{starting variable for the chain to be constructed}$$
$$S = \text{terminal variable at the end of the chain}$$
$$LHC = \text{resulting vector containing the skeleton index}$$
$$Fail = \text{logical variable set to } \textbf{True} \text{ if the procedure cannot construct}$$
$$\text{a chain}$$

In the algorithm an initial test is made by using the *Connect* table to see if a left-hand chain from α to S exists. If there is such a chain $(\alpha, \xi_1, \xi_2, \ldots, S)$, there exists a production of the form

$$\alpha \rightarrow \xi_1 \cdots \qquad :I$$

and so the entry

	Index	*Term*
	.	
	.	
	.	
N:	I	ξ_1
	.	
	.	
	.	

must be in the production table for α, say at location N in the table. To find the next term in the left-hand chain from α to S, then, the production table for ξ_1 is searched for some entry I such that

$$Connect(Term(\xi_1, I), S) = \textbf{True}$$

That is, a left descendant of ξ_1, $Term(\xi_1, I)$, is found which connects with S through a left-hand chain.

In general, when the algorithm has found the intermediate node ξ_k, an entry I is sought in the production table for ξ_k such that

$$Connect(Term(\xi_k, I), S) = \textbf{True}$$

Of course, if $Term(\xi_k, I) = S$, we are done; the algorithm terminates.

There is a final problem. Suppose that there is a left-recursive production with ξ_k, a variable in the left-hand chain, as the root. The production has the structure

$$\xi_k \rightarrow \xi_k \cdot \cdot \cdot \qquad :j$$

Depending on the order of entries in the production table, it would be possible to come first on an entry of the following form.

Index   Term

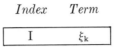

If so, since a left-hand chain does exist from ξ_k to S, ξ_k will again be added to the partially completed chain.   The algorithm is in an infinite loop adding an arbitrary number of ξ_k's to the partial chain, forever sure it is on the right track but never getting anywhere.

Definition 5.4:   A production set is called *left recursive* if there exists a possible left-hand chain generated by it from the sentence variable σ to some terminal symbol S

$$(\sigma, \xi_1, \xi_2, \ldots, \xi_n, S)$$

such that there are two distinct symbols ξ_i and ξ_j in the chain, which are the same.

To avoid problems of the sort mentioned above, the algorithm described here will assume that the grammar is not left recursive. This restriction does not limit the languages at all; and, especially since right recursion is allowed, no pernicious effect on the semantics has been noted.

Figure 5.5 shows a simple left-hand-chain generation algorithm in flow-chart form.   In addition to the variables noted above there are four variables internal to the algorithm.

τ holds the value of the last symbol added to the chain.
β is the symbol being tested in the search of a production table.
I is the location being tested in the production table.
J indexes through *LHC* as it is built.

5.4   the extended chain algorithm

It is not hard to show that the left-hand chain generated by the previous algorithm is the first, in lexicographic order, of all legal left-hand chains from α to S. In order to use the algorithm in the top-down parsing routine, however, it is necessary to extend it.   Since

$Chain(\alpha, S, LHC, Fail)$

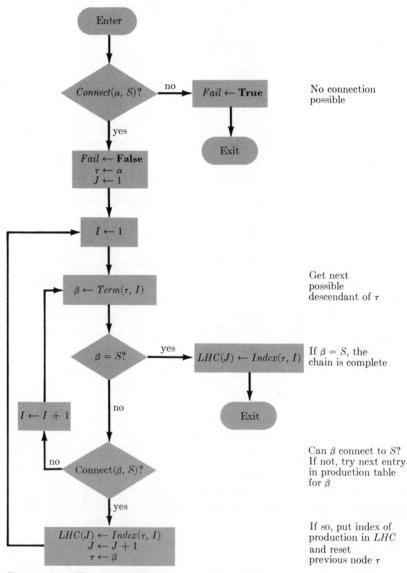

Figure 5.5   The *Chain* algorithm

the top-down parse searches through many possible skeletons, **Chain** must find the next skeleton after a given one.

Suppose that such an extended procedure exists and that the most recent output from it is a string of production indices $(i_1, i_2, \cdots i_n)$ representing some left-hand chain from α to S. The next possible chain in lexicographic order is at least n terms long, and starts with terms i_1 through i_{n-1}. Its index is

$$(i_1, i_2, \ldots , i_{n-1}, i_1', i_2', \ldots , i_m')$$

In other words, the search for the next left-hand chain begins by trying to replace the last link in the previous one. That is, if the old chain is

$$(\alpha, \beta_2, \ldots , \beta_{n-1}, S)$$

the next step is to establish a new link from β_{n-1} to S with a production sequence in which the first entry follows that for production i_n in the production table for β_{n-1}.

In order to find in the production table for β_{n-1} the next production that connects to S through a left-hand chain (if, indeed, such a production exists), it would be helpful to know where the entry for production i_n was found. This item of information will be called the *Key* and associated with the left-hand-chain vector will be a *Key* vector where *Key* (k) is the location of the k-th production of the chain in the production table for β_{k-1}.

Suppose, for example, we have the following production tables

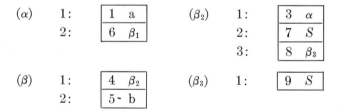

Suppose, further, that the *Index* of the last left-hand chain from α to S generated by the algorithm was (6, 4, 7). Then the *Key* is (2, 1, 2), since production 6 is in location 2, production 4 is in location 1, and production 7 is in location 2.

When the procedure is reentered, it starts looking for another chain it can forge from β_2 to S, since β_2 is the next to last node. Such a chain exists, in this example. It is found, by incrementing the last item of *Key*, and looking to see if *Connect* (*Term* $(\beta_2, 3), S)$ = **True.** Since there is a connection, β_3 is extended as the next term in the chain; the production table for β_3 is examined; and the chain is completed. So, next time around the left-hand-chain *Index* is (6, 4, 8, 9), and the *Key* is (2, 1, 3, 1).

A final comment, before proceeding to the algorithm itself, is to point out that the algorithm can now fail by exhausting the possibilities of chains. That is, we now have to take into account the possibility of failure during the process, whereas in the first algorithm the possibility only needed to be checked at the first step. A **True** at that point guaranteed success of the search since it promised a chain would exist.

In the following procedures, again:

α is the root of the left-hand chain, and is a variable.

S is the terminal symbol.

LHC at input is the last chain produced; at output, it contains the new chain.

Fail is the Boolean flag set to **True** if the routine fails.

Key is the companion to *LHC* and indicates the location of the production in the production table.

Length is the length of both *LHC* and *Key*. It is 0 on the first entry to the routine.

Given the index *I* of the production, *Root(I)* will generate the root of production *I*.

Now, let us look at the modified algorithm. First, it will be presented in an informal program-like sketch, then in the form of a flow chart.

Algorithm: Next-Chain (α, S, LHC, Fail, Key, Length)

Next-Chain 1:   **If** *Length* $\neq$ 0 **Then Go to** *Next-Chain 2;* **Else**
           If *Connect(α, S)* = **False Then**
                   Fail ← **True;**
           Else *Fail* ← **False;** *Temp* ← α; *I* ← 1;
           Go to *Next-Chain 3;*

(If this is the first time in the algorithm, check to see if a connection exists from α to *S*. If so, initialize the search to look for the first chain.)

Next-Chain 2:   *Last-Link* ← *LHC(Length);*
           Temp ← *Root(Last-Link);*
           I ← *Key(Length)* + 1;

(Since this is not the first time, initialize search at the last variable in the chain.)

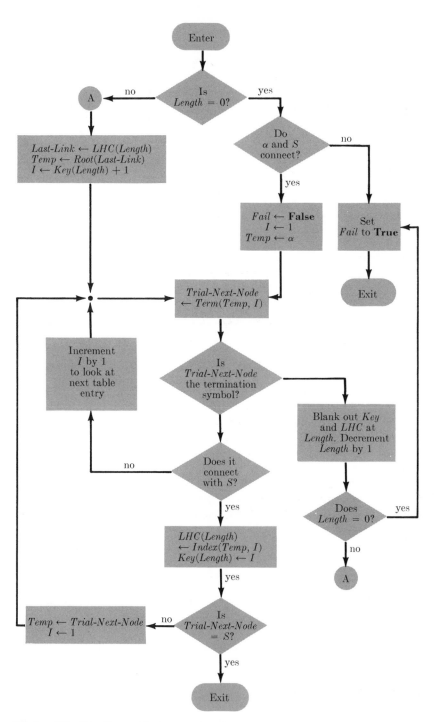

Figure 5.6 The *Next-Chain* algorithm flow chart

Next-Chain 3:   Trial-Next-Node ← *Term(Temp, I);*
                  If *Trial-Next-Node* = x **Then Go to** *Next-Chain 5;*
                  If *Trial-Next-Node* = *S* **Then Go to** *Next-Chain 6;*
                  If *Connect(Trial-Next-Node, S)* = **True Then**
                  Go to *Next-Chain 4; I* ← *I* + 1;
                  Repeat *Next-Chain 3;*

(This inner part of the algorithm searches for a continuation from the node *Temp* to *S*, by searching the *Temp* production table for a *Term* that connects with it. *Next-Chain 5* deals with failure of the search, *Next-Chain 4* with success, and *Next-Chain 6* with completion of the *Next-Chain.*)

Next-Chain 4:   LHC(Length) ← *Index(Temp, I);*
                  Temp ← *Trial-Next-Node;*
                  Key(Length) ← *I;*
                  Length ← *Length* + 1;
                  I ← 1; **Go to** *Next-Chain 3;*

(The successful production is added to the chain and the procedure continues on to seek the next node.)

Next-Chain 5:   Key(Length) ← 0;
                  LHC(Length) ← 0;
                  Length ← *Length* − 1;
                  If *Length* ≠ 0, **Go to** *Next-Chain 2;*
                  Fail ← **True; Exit;**

(Since it is not possible to continue the chain from the last node of the tree, the procedure goes back one link and starts over, looking for a chain. If it is impossible to go back any more, the attempt to build a *Next-Chain* has failed.)

Next-Chain 6:   LHC(Length) ← *Index(Temp, I);*
                  Key(Length) ← *I;* **Exit;**

(The next *LHC* has been found; the procedure outputs it and exits.)

Figure 5.6 shows the flow diagram for the **Next-Chain** algorithm.

problems

1. Transform each of the translation trees in Figure 5.7 to a binary tree and show its skeleton.

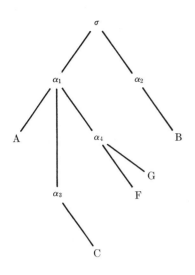

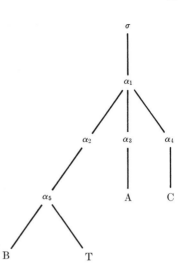

(a)   (b)

Figure 5.7   Translation trees
(a) and (b) for Problem 1

2.   Given the production set

$$\Pi_1 = \{\sigma \rightarrow \alpha\beta\alpha \qquad :1$$
$$\alpha \rightarrow \gamma A \qquad :2$$
$$\alpha \rightarrow B\alpha \qquad :3$$
$$\beta \rightarrow C\gamma \qquad :4$$
$$\gamma \rightarrow D \qquad :5$$
$$\gamma \rightarrow \alpha D \qquad :6\}$$

(a) Show two different skeletons from σ to a sentence starting with
the symbol D.

(b) Construct the indices of these skeletons and order them.

3.   Repeat Problem 2 with the production set below:

$$\Pi_2 = \{\sigma \rightarrow \alpha\beta\alpha \qquad :1$$
$$\sigma \rightarrow \xi\upsilon \qquad :2$$
$$\alpha \rightarrow \gamma A \qquad :3$$
$$\beta \rightarrow C\gamma \qquad :4$$
$$\gamma \rightarrow D \qquad :5$$
$$\xi \rightarrow \upsilon \qquad :6$$
$$\upsilon \rightarrow D\sigma\gamma \qquad :7\}$$

4. Construct the production tables for the production sets Π_1 and Π_2 of Problems 2 and 3.

5. (*a*) Construct the production tables for the simple arithmetic-expression grammar G_A presented in Chapter 3.

   (*b*) Which terminal symbols in G_A could be initial elements of legal sentences in $\Lambda(G_A)$?

   (*c*) Construct the possible skeletons for each terminal symbol and list them in order.

6. Is either production set Π_1 or Π_2 in Problems 2 and 3 above left recursive? Show why or why not in each case.

7. (Each chapter from now on will have a problem analogous to this one. It is, of course, the main exercise for this chapter.)

   (*a*) Implement an algorithm that takes as input a set of productions and constructs production tables.

   (*b*) Implement the **Next-Chain** algorithm so that it uses the production tables generated by the program written in Problem 7(a).

6

the top-down parse

Now that we have the procedure to develop the left-hand chains, the top-down parse procedure can be developed. All construction of the tree takes place in the **Next-Chain** procedure, since every node in the tree except for the root is eventually in some skeleton descended from some other node. The main procedure handles the bookkeeping and scheduling calls to **Next-Chain.** If it returns a *Fail* signal, then the main procedure has the responsibility of finding and trying the next possible skeleton structure.

This chapter presents the top-down parsing routine in quite a bit of detail since many of the concepts used here will be used later in developing other algorithms. It should also be repeated that this is only one possible algorithm out of many.

6.1   sequencing of chain searches

The sequencing of chains built is determined by the order of nodes in the skeleton. As an example, for the string $S_1S_2 \cdots S_8$, suppose a skeleton from α to S_1 has been generated as in Figure 6.1. Each S_i, for $2 \leq i \leq 8$, is in a subtree descended from one and only one of the

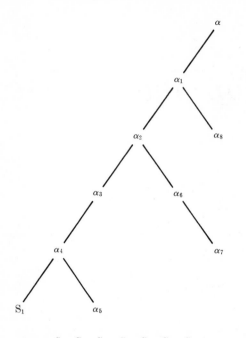

S_2 S_3 S_4 S_5 S_6 S_7 S_8

Figure 6.1   A sample partial
translation tree

nodes α_5, α_6, α_7, or α_8.   Also notice that the descendants of α_5 are to
the left of those of α_6 which are, in turn, to the left of those of α_7, and
so on.   It is not hard to show this fact if we recall that two phrases
(sets of symbols descended from a single node) either intersect completely or not at all.   That is, either one phrase completely contains
the other or they are completely separate.

Therefore there now is a series of new tasks—building subtrees
from each node to the terminal string starting with the node α_5.   The
subtree from α_5 to a string starting with S_2 must be finished next since
only then is the full phrase produced by α_5 known, and thus a starting point for the phrase produced by α_6 determined.   Suppose, for example, that the subtree from α_5 to the string is completed.   Then the
partially filled in tree might look as shown in Figure 6.2.   The next
step, then, is to try and connect the node α_6 with the terminal substring
starting at S_4.

Notice the *recursive* property of this algorithm.   Construction of
a subtree from the node α_5 to a terminal string $S_2 \cdots$ is a repetition
of the original task to construct a tree from σ to $S_1 S_2 \cdots S_8$.   There
could easily be several levels to this recursiveness.   Suppose the subtree from α_5 to $S_2 \cdots$ had a more complex structure than shown

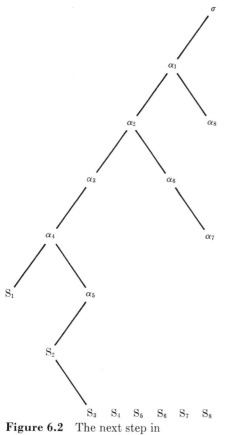

Figure 6.2   The next step in
producing a translation tree

above, for example, the pattern in Figure 6.3(a). The task of constructing the subtree starts out again by generating the skeleton in
Figure 6.3(b), but we are now faced with the necessity of construct-
ing a still deeper subtree, that is, one from α_{10} to $S_3 \cdot \cdot \cdot$. In this
case, the generation is trivial, but we have still started fresh tree gen-
erations three times. In each case, the succeeding generation must be
completed before the previous one can continue.

6.2   *data structure*

The algorithm requires three main storage regions. Naturally there
is an *Input* string of terminal symbols and an *Outlist* stack to store

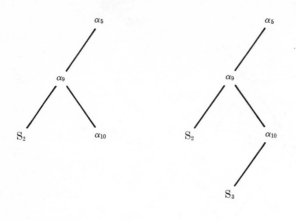

Figure 6.3   Deeper levels of
skeleton production

a representation of the completed parse. In addition, the algorithm
needs to store temporarily the nodes from which subtrees must be
generated. They are stored in a push-down stack called *Rootstack*.

Remember that a push-down stack is a data structure in which
the last item stored is on top and is the first item out. This type
of temporary storage is for recursive procedures, and is the temporary
data for a new task. The temporary data can be stored on top of
the data for an older task, and deleted when the new task is
done. The old task is then returned to with the data unchanged.

When the skeleton for σ to S_1 is built for the example above,
Rootstack is filled from the right as follows.

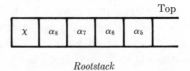

Rootstack

Once again, the symbol χ designates the end of the list. Subtrees
are now constructed from the nodes in *Rootstack* as they appear
during processing on the top of the stack to the terminal string. But,
remember that in the example the process of generating a tree from
α_5 to S_2 resulted in still another skeleton and set of nodes from which
to generate trees. Since the α_5 subtree must be complete before moving on to α_6, the procedure must immediately start looking for these

new subtrees.   The new nodes (in this example only one) are merely stuffed on top, so now *Rootstack* looks as follows.

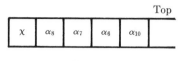

Rootstack

Suppose, in a more general case, that an attempt to construct a subtree fails somewhere in the middle of a parse.   That is, let *Rootstack* be

Rootstack

where the nodes labeled β_i are nodes in a subtree descended from some node α_j.   Now if the attempt to build a subtree from α_j fails in the middle, there may be some β's left on the stack that need to be erased in order to return to the previous state.   Thus it is necessary to designate in the *Rootstack* the *boundary* between those nodes that are associated with the newly aborted subtree development and those associated with the previous, interrupted attempt.   This boundary is designated by the symbol $\vdash$.   A similar boundary is needed for unstacking *Outlist* when the translator retreats from a failure to construct the subtree.   This symbol is designated by $\dashv$.   This new symbol implies that the entries following it in *Outlist* are subordinate to the preceding left-hand chain.   This way we know when no more backtracking can be done within a given skeleton, and the procedure must retreat still further by deleting the skeleton and attempting to construct another.   Thus $\dashv$ is inserted in *Outlist* whenever a new skeleton is found, and $\vdash$ is put on *Rootstack* under the new nodes in the skeleton.

For example, suppose the subtree in Figure 6.4 has been partially constructed.   The data appears at this stage as follows.

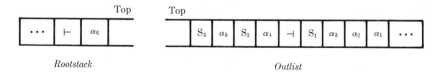

Rootstack   *Outlist*

The task now is to build a chain from α_6 to S_4.   Suppose no such tree exists.   The procedure backs up.   Since the other nodes, α_5 and α_4,

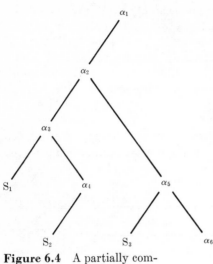

Figure 6.4   A partially completed tree

might have other subtree structures, we do not yet need to discard the entire skeleton rooted at α_1. So the previous chain, $S_3\alpha_5$, is unloaded, and the processor tries to build another chain from α_5 to S_3. But, no luck, suppose no such chain exists. The procedure backtracks again and unloads the next chain from *Outlist*. We now have the following structure.

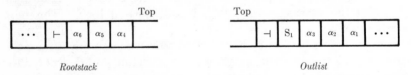

Now suppose no more possible chains exist from α_4 to S_2. We retreat again and find that we have stepped back through all of the nodes of the skeleton rooted at α_1. How do we know? Because a $\dashv$ is on top of *Outlist*. So all of the contents of *Rootstack* down through the $\vdash$ must be deleted. The next chain in *Outlist* is then deleted, storing the root α_1 in *Rootstack* in order to start looking for another left-hand chain.

6.3   the top-down algorithm

The flow chart for the top-down algorithm is shown in Figure 6.5. It has three major segments marked in the figure. Segment I (not counting the initialization) looks for the next root to be connected with the next free *Input* symbol in a subtree. The nodes are stored in *Rootstack*. If the symbol at the top of *Rootstack* is a terminal symbol, it is matched directly with *Input*. If it matches it is then put on the *Outlist;* if not, *Backtract* is called. This routine arranges the retreat from the unsuccessful attempt. Segment II calls *Next-Chain*, checks for success and, depending on the result, either calls *Backtrack* or outputs the resulting left-hand chain. Finally, segment III checks for the end of the procedure. Only if both *Rootstack* and *Input* are used up is the routine over. If either of these two cases occurs by itself, an invalid tree has been built, and *Backtrack* is called to the rescue again.

Figure 6.6 shows a flow chart for the *Outresults* section of the algorithm. This module writes the left-hand chain along with its associated data on the *Outlist*. If there are any nodes in the skeleton of the chain that are unattached to the *Input* string, they are stored in *Rootlist* so they can be examined in the proper order. Remember that the nodes of a skeleton are attached to the *Input* string in order from the bottom right-hand chain to top, from the leftmost character in each chain to the right. Since *Rootstack* is a last-in, first-out structure, the nodes in the skeleton are stored from the top right-hand chain to the bottom, from the right to left within each chain.

For example, suppose the skeleton in Figure 6.7 has been found from α to S_i. The order in which the nodes would be examined as roots of subtrees is, written left to right,

$$\gamma_1 \gamma_2 \gamma_3 \gamma_4 \gamma_5$$

Thus they must be pushed down in *Rootstack* successively from right to left. In that way, γ_1 will end up on top of the stack, with γ_2 next, and so on to γ_5 at the bottom.

From examination of the top-down algorithm, then, we can see that at any time the *Outlist* is either headed by

1. A left-hand chain, terminated by a $\dashv$, such as

$$\dashv S_i \alpha_1 \alpha_2 \cdots \alpha_n$$

2. A full subtree, terminated by $\vdash$, such as

$$\vdash \dashv S_i \alpha_1 \alpha_2 \cdots \alpha_n \cdots \dashv S_j \beta_1 \cdots$$

3. A terminal symbol, standing as a subtree from a node, this node being the terminal symbol itself

$$S_i \cdots$$

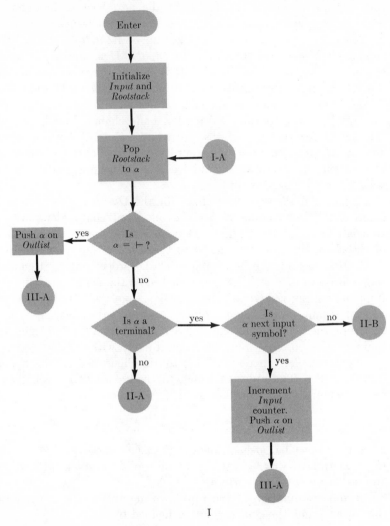

Figure 6.5 A flow chart for
the top-down algorithm

When the subroutine *Backtrack* starts to unpack *Outlist* looking
for the last left-hand chain that can be deleted, it confronts the above
three possibilities.   A terminal symbol cannot, of course, have another
tree from it; it stands for itself.   So *Backtrack* merely ignores it and
moves on.   If it reaches a ⊢, the next sequence must either be a left-
hand chain, a subtree, or a ⊣.   Every left-hand chain from a variable
symbol to a terminal symbol is terminated by a ⊣.   So the routine

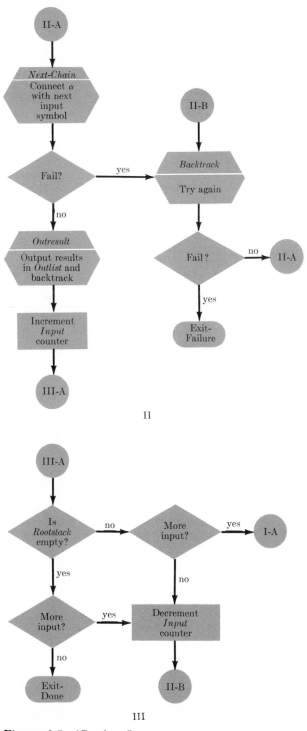

II

III

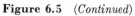

Figure 6.5 (*Continued*)

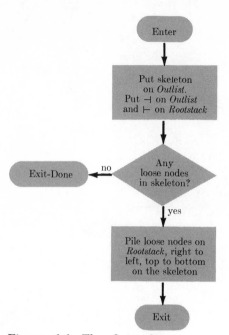

Figure 6.6 The *Outresults* flow chart

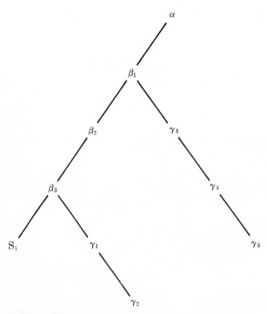

Figure 6.7 A skeleton from α to S_i

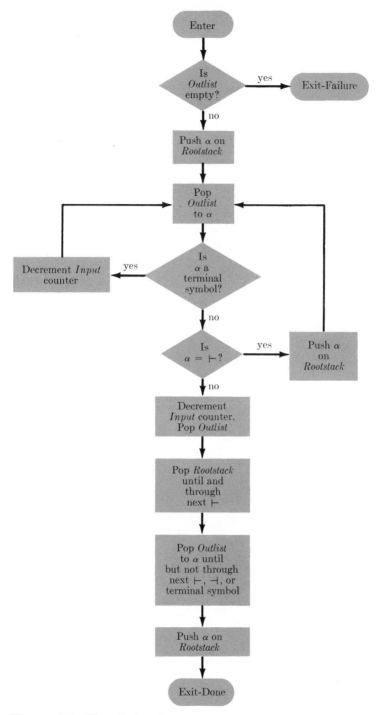

Figure 6.8 The *Backtrack*
flow chart

moves back through *Outlist* until a ⊣ is found.   Figure 6.8 shows a flow chart of *Backtrack*.

6.4   ambiguity of the output

Each time the algorithm finds a skeleton from a node to a terminal character, the left-hand chain, the backbone of the skeleton is output on *Outlist*.   If the node itself is a terminal symbol S, the chain is one term long.

Look at the preorder walk of the translation tree shown in Figure 6.9 in terms of its left-hand chains

$$\sigma\alpha_1\alpha_2 S_1 \mid S_2 \mid \alpha_3 S_3 \mid S_4 \mid \alpha_4 S_5 \mid \alpha_5\alpha_6 S_6 \mid \alpha_7 S_7 \mid S_8$$

The vertical bars separate it into a sequence of left-hand chains that terminate with terminal characters.   This pattern is also the pattern produced by the translation routine (with the left-hand chains reversed in order).   The output string built up from the top-down parsing routine is the preorder walk of the translation tree.

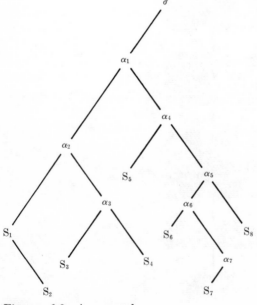

Figure 6.9   An example translation tree

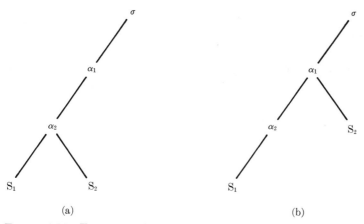

(a)   (b)

Figure 6.10   Two trees with
the same preorder walk

However, the walk is ambiguous.   The same string can represent
the preorder walk of different trees.   For example, look at the two
trees in Figure 6.10.   The preorder walks of these trees are both
$\sigma\alpha_1\alpha_2 S_1 S_2$.   Thus, although the two left-hand strings can be identified
as $\sigma\alpha_1\alpha_2 S_1$ and S_2, the placement of the second chain is ambiguous.

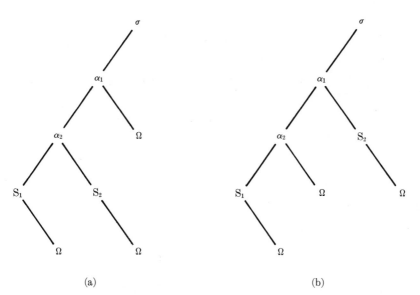

(a)   (b)

Figure 6.11   Augmented trees
having different preorder walks

We can recognize the end of a left-hand chain because it is signaled by a terminal symbol that cannot have a left descendant. But right-hand chains do not have recognizable terminating symbols.

Let us introduce one and designate it as Ω. Now, assuming that Ω is not in either the variable or terminal-symbol set (that is, it is a new symbol), it can be attached to the end of each right-hand side of a production. It is carried through the parsing routine by assuming that it always connects to a null element between S_i and S_{i+1}, and it will appear in the output string as another one-symbol left-hand chain. But it also designates the end of a right-hand chain. The trees in the example above then become transformed into the trees in Figure 6.11. And the preorder walks of the trees are, respectively,

$$\sigma\alpha_1\alpha_2 S_1\Omega S_2\Omega\Omega$$
and
$$\sigma\alpha_1\alpha_2 S_1\Omega\Omega S_2\Omega$$

Now, by using this new convention, the tree can be reconstructed from *Outlist*. Thus *Outlist* contains all structural information embedded in the translation tree, and it can form the direct input to an interpreter or compiler.

problems

1. Rewrite the top-down algorithm (including *Backtrack*) to incorporate the Ω symbol in the processing.

2. Develop an algorithm for reconstructing the tree from an *Outlist* representation.

3. Write a translator based on the top-down algorithm discussed in this chapter.

7

the bottom-up parse

Since a top-down parsing algorithm was described in Chapter 6, it seems only fair for symmetry that bottom-up parsing be discussed next. Such a parsing algorithm does, in fact, exist, and it is important, both in its own right as a general technique and as a motivation for some of the special subclasses of languages we will study later. Most of these classes are designed to make the bottom-up parse, or some version of it, more efficient.

The top-down parse was so named because, given the basic initial picture below,

σ

S_1 S_2 S_3 $\cdots$ S_n

the procedure attempts to build left-hand chains down from possible nodes, starting with σ. The first step results in the partial binary tree shown in Figure 7.1.

The bottom-up parsing algorithm starts with the same picture, but tries to build the tree by finding the lowest subtrees first, connecting them to form a new string, a sentential form. The result from the first step in a bottom-up translation of the string might look

99

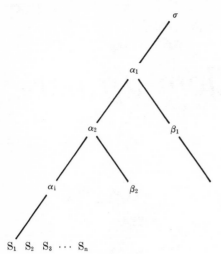

Figure 7.1 A translation tree partially completed by the top-down parse

like the tree in Figure 7.2. The new string input to the translator in that case is the old string with $S_3 S_4 S_5$ replaced by the root of the phrase α:

$$S_1 S_2 \alpha S_1 \cdots S_n$$

7.1   searching for handles

In Chapter 4 the *handle* of a sentential form was defined to be the leftmost prime phrase in the form, where a *prime phrase* is a phrase containing no other phrases within it. The symbols in a prime phrase

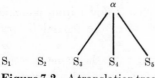

Figure 7.2 A translation tree partially completed by the bottom-up parse

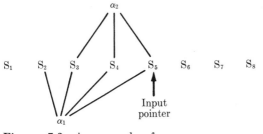

Figure 7.3 An example of search for handle

all descend from a single node, as has been illustrated for the phrase $S_3S_4S_5$. Analogously to the top-down parse, the bottom-up algorithm is based on reading one input symbol at a time from left to right. Thus, if the algorithm is geared to searching for a prime phrase, the one it finds will be the handle; or, rather, a candidate for the handle. Just as in the top-down parse, *potential* left-hand chains were generated, *potential* handles are found by the bottom-up translator.

At each step as the processor moves through the input string, it tries to find a handle terminating at that point. Figure 7.3 illustrates this process. The processor is now at S_5 in the input string. There are two substrings terminating at S_5; one is from a production

$$\alpha_1 \rightarrow S_2S_3S_4S_5 \qquad :i_1$$

and the other is from a production

$$\alpha_2 \rightarrow S_3S_4S_5 \qquad :i_2$$

If there were a prime phrase terminating to the left of S_5, the algorithm would have found it and processed it. Thus, either there is no possible phrase to the left of S_5, or, if one exists, it has been discovered, tried, and discarded as not leading to a correct translation. The order in which the two phrases are tried is immaterial. Assuming that the productions are ordered in some way, they can be tried in that order.

7.2 *substitution and backtrack*

Suppose production i_1 is chosen first. The subtree is output and an α_1 is substituted in the input string, which is now

$$S_1\alpha_1S_6S_7S_8$$

The input marker is still looking at the symbol to the left of S_6.   Now, can there be a potential handle that terminates to the left of the input pointer?   No, for if it exists now, it would have existed prior to the substitution.   On the other hand, α_1 is a new symbol, so a new phrase terminating with α_1 on its right is possible.   So the input pointer starts out at the same place, the symbol to the left of S_6.   Suppose no prime phrase is found ending at α, or any symbols to the right of it.   The procedure needs to backtrack and restore the previous phrase it has filled in, but what was the previous substitution?   There is a beautifully simple answer.   Since no later substitution can be made to the left of a previous substitution, the *most recent substitution must be represented by the rightmost variable symbol in the partially reduced input string.*   If the index of the production is stored in the output list or with the variable symbol in the input string, it is a simple matter to find the next possible phrase.

7.3   example of bottom-up parse

Let us look at a very simple example of backtracking in the bottom-up parse.   An elementary production set for some simple arithmetic expressions is shown below.

$$\{\langle arithmetic\ expression \rangle \rightarrow A + \langle primary \rangle \qquad :1$$
$$\langle primary \rangle \rightarrow A \qquad :2$$
$$\langle primary \rangle \rightarrow A \times \langle primary \rangle \qquad :3\}$$

Take a simple sentence in the language.

$$\bar{s} = A + A \times A$$

The general translation tree for $\bar{s}$ is shown in Figure 7.4.   The first *possible* handle of $\bar{s}$ is the first occurrence of A on the left, even though the actual handle of the tree is the rightmost A.   Thus an initial attempt at bottom-up parsing would conjecture that the new sentential form in the canonical production sequence would be

$$\langle primary \rangle + A \times A$$

The other two A's would also be converted to $\langle primary \rangle$'s and the processor would then run out of possible primary phrases.

The entire process is described below as a sequence of sentential forms.   Backtrack steps are indicated with a (**B**) on the right side

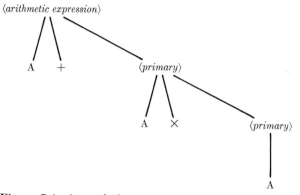

Figure 7.4   A translation tree
for A + A × A

of the string, and the previously tried handle is underlined.   The
reader should understand why each step follows from the previous
one.

1. A + A × A
2. ⟨*primary*⟩ + A × A
3. ⟨*primary*⟩ + ⟨*primary*⟩ × A
4. ⟨*primary*⟩ + ⟨*primary*⟩ × ⟨*primary*⟩
5. ⟨*primary*⟩ + ⟨*primary*⟩ × A̲   (**B**)

　　　Line 4 has no handles.   The previous string is restored (the last
handle tried is underlined).   But there are no other handles in this
new string.

6. ⟨*primary*⟩ + A̲ × A   (**B**)
7. ⟨*primary*⟩ + A̅ × ⟨*primary*⟩
8. ⟨*primary*⟩ + ⟨*primary*⟩
9. ⟨*primary*⟩ + A̲ ×̲⟨*primary*⟩ -   (**B**)
10. ⟨*primary*⟩ + A × A̲   (**B**)
11. A̲ + A × A   (**B**)
12. A + ⟨*primary*⟩ × A
13. A + ⟨*primary*⟩ × ⟨*primary*⟩
14. A + ⟨*primary*⟩ × A̲   (**B**)
15. A + A̲ × A   (**B**)
16. A + A̅ × ⟨*primary*⟩
17. A + ⟨*primary*⟩
18. ⟨*arithmetic expression*⟩

7.4 data structures

Operating data for the translation algorithm are held in three push-down stacks, one for input, one for output, and one for temporary holding. They are labeled, respectively, *Inlist, Outlist,* and *Holdlist.* Their relationship can be visualized in terms of a railroad switching yard, as shown in Figure 7.5. Symbols are moved from *Inlist* to *Holdlist* one by one. The *comparator* window checks to see if the right-hand side of *Holdlist* contains a possible prime phrase. If a possible handle is found, it is moved out onto *Outlist.*

Each of these lists has a different special structural property to it. *Inlist* is the simplest, a simple string of terminal symbols treated as a stack with the stack top on the left. As the stack is popped, the input string is read from left to right. When a possible handle is found and its root is stored in place of it in *Holdlist,* the routine wants to store the index of the production with the variable symbol. In that way, if a backtrack is necessary at that root, the search routine will know where to start looking. *Holdlist,* then, has two items for each entry. If the symbol is terminal, then the second item is 0; if it is a variable, the second item is the index of the production reducing to it. So *Holdlist* might look as follows:

Symbol	B	γ	α	A
Index	0	I_2	I_1	0

When backtracking, the last prime phrase is unloaded from *Outlist* and stored back on *Holdlist.* The structure of *Outlist* must contain all of the data stored in *Holdlist* and thus the double entry is, again, the rule. There is one more modification, however. The procedure must be able to distinguish successive phrases in *Outlist,* so an extra symbol ⊣ is once again introduced as a spacer between phrases as they are output on the stack.

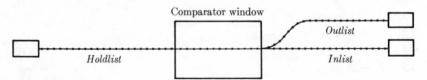

Figure 7.5 Bottom-up parse stacks viewed as a switching system

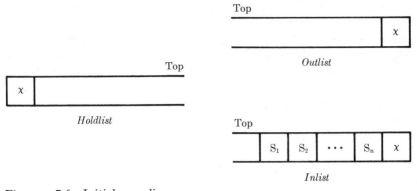

Figure 7.6 Initial conditions for bottom-up parse

7.5   the bottom-up algorithm

The algorithm starts processing with the entire input string stored in *Inlist*. The two other stacks, *Holdlist* and *Outlist*, are empty as shown in Figure 7.6. At the end of a successful parse, *Inlist* is empty, *Outlist* contains a sequence of symbol strings separated by ⊣'s, and *Holdlist* contains the sentence variable σ, since that must be the final reduction in a bottom-up parse (see Figure 7.7).

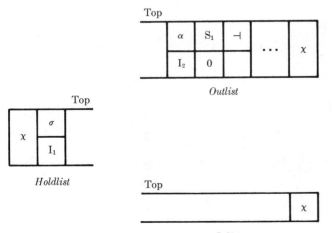

Figure 7.7 Terminal conditions for successful parse

One other possible final condition is that in which the backtracking fails. This condition would be met if *Holdlist* is empty when the backtracking algorithm wants to search it for a possible variable. Since *Holdlist* is empty, *Outlist* must also be empty and *Inlist* must again contain the whole sentence. That is, the configuration returns to the initial conditions.

The algorithm is quite straightforward and simple in form. Its flow chart is exhibited in Figure 7.8 while a more informal description is also made.

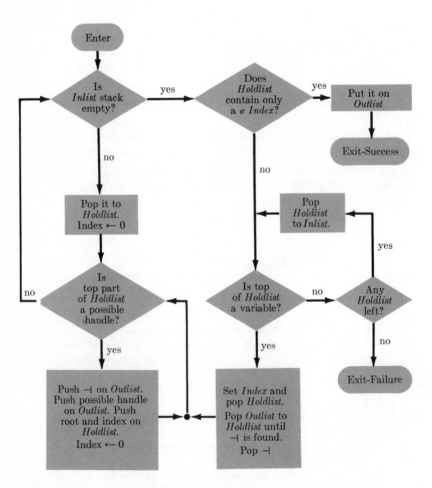

Figure 7.8 A flow chart for the bottom-up parse

Algorithm: Bottom-Up

BUP1:   (Get next input symbol) **If** *Inlist* empty **Then Go to** *BUP4;*
          Else Pop *Inlist* **To** *Holdlist;*
          Index ← 0;

BUP2:   (Look for handle)   Search for a production after *Index* with an argument that matches a top substring of *Holdlist;*
          If none exists **Then Go to** *BUP1;*

BUP3:   (Output possible handle)   **Pop** the matched substring **From** *Holdlist* **To** *Outlist;*
          Push the root and index of the matched production **On** *Holdlist;*
          Index ← 0;
          Go to *BUP2;*

BUP4:   (Check if done)   **If** *Holdlist* contains only a $\sigma/\langle index\ term \rangle$ on top and nothing else below **Then Exit**–Success;

BUP5:   (Backtrack) **Pop** *Holdlist* **To** *Inlist* **Until** a $\langle variable \rangle$ $\langle production\ index \rangle$ pair is on top of *Holdlist;*
          If none **Then Exit**–Failure;
          Else Pop *Holdlist;*
          Index ← the $\langle production\ index \rangle;$
          Pop *Outlist* **To** *Holdlist* **Until** a ⊣ is found;
          Pop *Outlist;*
          Go to *BUP2;*

7.6   reconstruction

One final question that should be answered is whether *Outlist* contains all necessary information about the translation tree. That is, could the original sentence be reconstructed from *Outlist?* Remember that, in the case of the top-down parse, an additional symbol was needed to make the output unambiguous. In the case of the bottom-up parse, however, this modification is not necessary. The backtrack process itself re-creates previous sentential forms, so the reconstruction is merely a recursive adaptation of backtrack.

Algorithm: Reconstruct

REC1:   Let $\bar{s}_i$ be the top phrase in *Outlist.*

REC2:   Let $\bar{s}_{i+1}$ be the result of substituting the next phrase in *Outlist* for the rightmost variable in $\bar{s}_i.$

REC3:   When *Outlist* is empty, the last sentential form constructed, $\bar{s}_m$, is the original input sentence.

When *Outlist* is read from bottom to top, the phrases are in proper order for an interpreter or compiler since the semantic translation is from the bottom up.

problems

1. Refer again to the grammar G_A presented in Chapter 3 and list all *possible* handles for the following sentences and sentential forms, assuming that you do not know at this time the structure of the final tree.

    (*a*) $A + A \times A$

    (*b*) $\langle term \rangle \langle multiplying\ operator \rangle \langle factor \rangle$

    (*c*) $\langle arithmetic\ expression \rangle + \langle arithmetic\ expression \rangle$

2. Let $\bar{a}$ and $\bar{b}$ be two possible handles of a sentential form $\bar{x}$ such that $\bar{a}$ and $\bar{b}$ correspond to different productions and $\bar{a}$ and $\bar{b}$ terminate at the same point in $\bar{x}$, that is,

    $$\bar{x} = \bar{y}_1 \bar{a} \bar{x}' = \bar{y}_2 \bar{b} \bar{x}'$$

    (*a*) Show that either $\bar{a}$ and $\bar{b}$ are of different length ($|\bar{a}| \neq |\bar{b}|$) or that $\bar{a}$ and $\bar{b}$ are identical and thus correspond with two productions having the same argument.

    (*b*) Show that either $\bar{a}$ is a substring of $\bar{b}$ or $\bar{b}$ is a substring of $\bar{a}$ (or both).

3. Suggest how the previous theorem can be applied to build a data structure that simplifies searching for handles, especially after a backtrack.   (Hint: Chains of productions ordered by inclusion of their arguments can be constructed.)

4. Step through the bottom-up algorithm, as was done in Section 7.3, for the following sentences in the language generated by the production set presented in Section 7.3.   Indicate the backtracking steps.

    (*a*) $A \times A$

    (*b*) $(A + A)$

5. Select a suitable data structure for a production set and develop a program that will search for a handle in the top of a push-down stack. Remember, the most important parameter governing your design this time is simplicity of the programming effort, since you are under a time constraint. Not completing an elegant design is far worse than completing an inefficient but operating program. Given that the design can be programmed on schedule, speed of operation then becomes an important parameter. Perhaps you can suggest others.

6. Use your search algorithm to write a program implementing the bottom-up parse.

8

the left-right parse

The final algorithm to be presented for parsing a sentence in a general context-free language appears to move horizontally, from left to right, as it constructs the translation tree in parallel. It could be called a *sideways* parse although it will be seen later to be more closely related to the top-down technique. A form of this algorithm was used by D. E. Knuth [16] to study the properties of a special class of grammars called LR(k) grammars, which will be examined in Chapter 9. J. Earley [11] has also studied the properties of a form of this algorithm, showing it to be an extremely efficient translation procedure for general context-free languages.

8.1 *intuitive description*

The two previous parsing algorithms required backtracking; that is, repeatedly comparing new partial phrase structures with the input string until, finally, a complete match is found. We might think of avoiding the backtracking activity by carrying along all possible partial trees. However, as was pointed out earlier, the number of possible trees is infinite. But, the number of non-left-recursive skeletons from a root to a terminal symbol is finite.   Since the translation tree is composed of skeletons, we might consider collecting for each terminal symbol in the input string all of the right-hand chains making up possible skeletons connecting a root to that symbol.

But, how does the translator know what a proper next root would be?   Let us consider only one possible tree, remembering that the process can be carried along for all possible trees simultaneously. Suppose a symbol S_i in the input string is being read.   All the previous symbols to the left have been read, and for each symbol a list of all the right-hand chains in possible skeletons from possible roots to that symbol has been established.   The substring read is

$$S_1S_2 \cdot \cdot \cdot S_{i-1}S_i$$

Now, either S_{i-1} is at the bottom of a skeleton (its *base*), with α at the top (its *root*), or it is embedded in a skeleton based at some previous S_k. The possible root for the skeleton to S_i is the symbol $\beta_{k,\sigma}$ in Figure 8.1(a) or $\beta_{m,2}$ in (b).

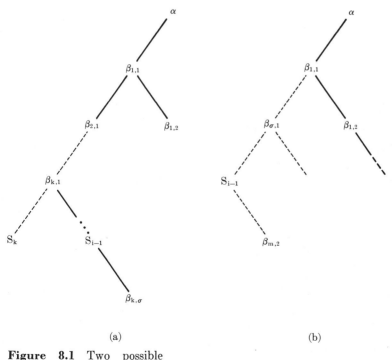

(a)   (b)

Figure   8.1   Two   possible positions for S_{i-1}

Suppose that, for each terminal symbol as read from left to right, information describing each possible skeleton connecting to that symbol is saved. At each step, the possible skeleton will be based on the partial trees constructed previously, since the root of the skeleton must be contained in the skeleton based at some previous terminal symbol. Constructing these sets for all possible skeletons throughout the input string will leave us, at the end, with only possible skeletons connecting the tree with the last terminal symbol in the *Input* string. Any complete tree still possible at the end is clearly a legitimate translation tree, and the tree can be found by tracing back through the information sets.

8.2   states and state sets

Now let us see how the parse actually works. First, these information sets will be defined formally, and then the algorithms for constructing them will be presented.

As the parser moves along the input string, it creates a set of information about the progress of the translation up to that point. This information is stored as a collection of elements called *states*. The states are not necessarily stored in any particular order, although, again, the programmer may choose some particular structure to facilitate his implementation. Reasonably enough, this collection of states is called a *state set*.

Each state contains information about a particular production whose right-hand side could still be a possible component of a translation tree. It can be seen that, for any nontrivial sentence, the state set at some intermediate point could contain several entries. Of course, the size of the state set depends on the complexity of the grammar and the complexity of the sentence being worked on.

There are three pieces of information contained in the state. First, the state is associated with a particular production, so the index of that production is in the state. Second, the state contains the number (perhaps 0) of steps that the translator has processed through the argument of the production in matching it with the input string. Finally, the state set contains information identifying that point where the translator started looking for a phrase in the parse. More formally, the state is defined as follows:

Definition 8.1: A *state* at point i of the input string is an ordered triple (p, n, m), where p is the index of a production, n is an integer where $0 \leq n \leq$ (the length of the argument of production p), and m is an integer where $1 \leq m \leq i$.

For convenience, the state is represented by writing the production p out, putting a dot at point n in the argument of p, and putting m after a colon following the production. Assume that the colon is not in the set of terminal symbols. If the colon is in the set, some other delimiter can be used. Thus a state is written as follows:

$$\alpha \rightarrow \bar{x} \cdot \bar{y} \qquad :m$$

where

$$\alpha \rightarrow \bar{x}\bar{y} \in \Pi$$

8.3   generation of state sets—direct

Now let us see how a state set is generated. Suppose the translator is at symbol X_i in scanning an input string n symbols long.

Scanner

↓

$X_1 X_2 \cdots X_{i-1} X_i X_{i+1} \cdots X_n$

The algorithm instructs us to build a state set S_i, using three generation rules.

The first rule, called *direct* generation, carries over modified entries from the state set S_{i-1}. Assume that state set S_{i-1} contains states corresponding to phrases still in the running. That is, suppose the state

$$\alpha \rightarrow \bar{y} \cdot X_i \bar{z} \qquad :m$$

is in S_{i-1}. This entry says there is a string of symbols $X_j \cdots X_{i-1}$ produced by the string $\bar{y}$, so this production is, through the phrase $\bar{y}$, a possible part of the translation tree. But X_i, the next symbol in the input string, matches the next symbol in the production, so the phrase is still a possible part of the tree at point i. Therefore

$$\alpha \rightarrow \bar{y}X_1 \cdot \bar{z} \qquad :m$$

is put in S_i. More formally, the concept is expressed as follows.

State Generation Rule 1 (Direct): Let $X_1 X_2 \cdots X_n$ be an input string, and $S_1, S_2, \ldots, S_n$ be the associated state sets. Then the state $\alpha \rightarrow \bar{y}A \cdot \bar{z} \qquad :m$ is in S_i, if and only if $\alpha \rightarrow \bar{y} \cdot A\bar{z} \qquad :m$ is in S_{i-1} and $A = X_i$.

8.4   generation of state sets—closure

Let us continue our examination of the state above, which was just put into S_i, and look closer at $\bar{z}$. Suppose, first, that $\bar{z}$ is not a null string. (The case of $\bar{z}$ being null is considered in Section 8.5.) Then

$$\bar{z} = a_1 a_2 \cdots a_k$$

If a_1 is a terminal character, we have the same case as before in constructing S_i directly. That is, the state will be modified and carried forward to S_{i+1} if $a_1 = X_{i+1}$, and will be eliminated from contention if $a_1 \neq X_{i+1}$. But that worry can be left to the construction of S_{i+1}. What if $a_1 = \xi$, a variable?

In that case, if we are to look for the occurrence of ξ in the terminal string, it must be as a new phrase. Since that new phrase starts at X_{i+1}, the translator must start by assuming that all possible phrases generated by ξ are in contention. Thus a state corresponding to each production in Π, which has ξ as the root, is added to S_i. If $\xi \rightarrow \bar{y}$ is such a production, then

$$\xi \rightarrow \cdot\, \bar{y} \qquad :i$$

is the state added to S_i. The dot in front of the argument indicates that the processor is just starting to look for the phrase $\bar{y}$, and the i indicates that the search for $\bar{y}$ was initiated in state set i. This operation is applied to every state in S_i, and is called the *closure* operation.

State Generation Rule 2 (Closure):   If

$$\alpha \rightarrow \bar{y} \cdot \xi \qquad :m$$

is in S_i, then

$$\xi \rightarrow \cdot\, \bar{a} \qquad :i$$

is inserted in S_i for all $\xi \rightarrow \bar{a}$ in Π.

Note that in the above operation the closure rule is applied to every state in S_i, not just the original states. That means that each new state added to S_i by closure becomes itself a candidate for that operation. For example, suppose that

$$\alpha \rightarrow A \cdot \xi B \qquad :m$$

is in S_i and that $\xi \rightarrow \gamma$ and $\gamma \rightarrow B$ are in the production set Π of the grammar. The closure operator on the state above means that

$$\xi \rightarrow \cdot\, \gamma \qquad :m$$

is added to S_i.   But now closure must also be applied to the new state, and so

$$\gamma \to \cdot \, \mathrm{B} \qquad :i$$

is also added to S_i.

A particular production state is only added once in a specific set, otherwise left recursion would rear its ugly head once again, and we would find ourselves building an unbounded state set.   For example, from the production

$$\gamma \to \gamma \mathrm{A}$$

an endless generation of the state

$$\gamma \to \cdot \, \gamma \mathrm{A} \qquad :i$$

would take place.

8.5   generation of state sets—indirect

The third and final generation rule for placing states in state sets, the *indirect* rule, is related to the first.   It is third because it is easier to understand in terms of closure.   Remember that, in the direct rule, a state is moved from S_{i-1} to S_i if the terminal symbol immediately to the right of the dot in the state matches the next symbol in the input string.   If the symbol immediately to the right of the dot in the state in S_{i-1} is a variable, the closure rule requires the introduction of new states to S_{i-1} in order to look for an occurrence of that variable as a phrase in the terminal string, starting at S_i.

Let us look at a diagram.   Suppose

$$\sigma \to \bar{\mathrm{y}} \cdot \xi \bar{\mathrm{z}} \qquad :r$$

is in S_{i-1}.   The situation might be schematized as in Figure 8.2. Up to S_{i-1}, the production $\sigma \to \bar{\mathrm{y}} \xi \bar{\mathrm{z}}$ is possibly a part of the translation tree.   That is, $\bar{\mathrm{y}}$ connects in a translation tree to a subphrase ending at X_{i-1} in the string $X_r \cdots X_{i-1}$.   In order for the production to continue being possible, ξ must connect next, through some tree, to a phrase starting at X_i.   Thus all productions with ξ as the root are put in S_{i-1} as states.

Suppose now that the translator has moved on, and at X_j in the input string the variable ξ is, indeed, shown to connect to a phrase from X_i to X_j.   How would this be indicated?   The dot would be at the end of the left-hand side of the state corresponding to the production.   The state would be

$$\xi \to \bar{\mathrm{v}} \cdot \qquad :i-1$$

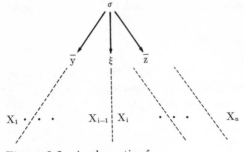

Figure 8.2 A schematic of a
partially completed left-right
parse

There are no more symbols to look for in this state. Now, just as
in the direct rule, a symbol ξ has been validated and found to be a
possible root in the translation tree. The state can only have been
introduced into the system by application of the closure rule, which
indicates that there is at least one state in S_{i-1} of the form

$$\sigma \to \bar{y} \cdot \xi\bar{z} \qquad :r$$

Now, at point j the ξ has been shown to conform to a phrase in the
sentence and so, in a step analogous to the direct generation, the state
above is carried forward to S_j with the indicator moved one more step
to the right, so the new state in S_j is

$$\sigma \to \bar{y}\xi \cdot \bar{z} \qquad :r$$

The use of the third element of the state is now apparent. It
refers back to the point in the input string where that state was first
introduced by the closure rule. The indirect rule can now be stated
formally.

State Generation Rule 3 (Indirect): Let state set S_i contain a state
of the following form

$$\xi \to \bar{v} \cdot \qquad :k$$

Then transform all states in S_k that are of the form

$$\sigma \to \bar{y} \cdot \xi\bar{z} \qquad :r$$

to

$$\sigma \to \bar{y}\xi \cdot \bar{z} \qquad :r$$

and add them to S_i.

8.6   the algorithm

Before starting the translation algorithm, two simple modifications to the input are necessary. The purpose of these modifications is to provide a formal means of detecting the end of the string and a means of starting the algorithm properly.

A new terminal symbol, $\dashv$, not used in the grammar, is attached on the right end of the input string. Thus, if the string of terminal symbols

$$X_1 X_2 \cdot \cdot \cdot X_n$$

is the original n-character input string, the string

$$X_1 X_2 \cdot \cdot \cdot X_n\dashv$$

is the new, modified $(n + 1)$-character input string.

Of course, now that a new symbol has been introduced in the grammar, the grammar needs to account for it.   Let G be the grammar where

$$G = (\Sigma, \, T, \, \Pi, \, \sigma)$$

Now σ is the starting variable.   Any terminal string produced by σ is a sentence in the grammar.   However, under the modification of the input string above, a legal sentence is now a terminal string produced by σ followed by a $\dashv$. How can this be incorporated in G?   Let σ' be a variable symbol not presently in T.   Then, by adding a new production of the form

$$\sigma' \rightarrow \sigma\dashv$$

to Π, any terminal string produced by σ' will become a legal sentence in the new form. The modified grammar is formally defined as follows:

$$G' = (\Sigma \cup \{\dashv\}, \, T \cup \{\sigma'\}, \, \Pi \cup \{\sigma' \rightarrow \sigma\dashv\}, \, \sigma')$$

These modifications do not change the language in any meaningful way.   The symbol $\dashv$ exists anyway in practice, depending on the language, as a carriage return, end-of-file mark, period, or other delimiter.   Otherwise, the input processor to the translator would never know when to stop looking for new symbols.   Whatever it is that causes the input processor to stop, then, will also cause it to transmit the message, "I just read a $\dashv$," to the translator.

The first step in the translation process is to build an initial state set S_0.   This set is constructed before reading the first input symbol. The first state put in it is

$$\sigma' \rightarrow \cdot \, \sigma\dashv \qquad :0$$

If, as has been stated before, the state set at a point tells which phrases the processor will start looking for at the next point in the input stream, the initial state can be intuitively understood to be saying that the translator is to look for a sentence in the language starting at the first input symbol.

Now S_0 can (in fact, must) be extended. The direct (Section 8.3) and indirect (Section 8.5) rules are not usable since they depend on a previous state set, and none exists. But the closure of S_0 can be constructed (Section 8.4).

The rest of the algorithm proceeds in a similar manner. To construct S_i, the direct rule is first applied to S_{i-1}. If there exists a legal parse of the input string, the direct rule must bring at least one state over into S_i. Then the indirect rule is applied repeatedly until all completed states have been treated. Finally, the closure rule is applied to the state set. The generation rules are applied in the following order, then, to build S_i:

1.   Direct generation from S_{i-1} (rule 1)
2.   Indirect generation (rule 3)
3.   Closure (rule 2)

8.7   states and skeletons

Since a state is a form of a production, it can be considered to be representative of a right-hand chain. Consider a possible skeleton of a translation tree from σ'. It is simple to show that every right-hand tree in the skeleton is represented in the state set, S_0. Note again that the state set is finite since the number of states cannot exceed the number of productions in Π, even though the number of skeletons may be infinite by means of left recursion. For instance, suppose the skeleton in Figure 8.3 is possible. The states

$$\sigma' \rightarrow \cdot\, \sigma\dashv \qquad :0$$
$$\sigma \rightarrow \cdot\, \alpha_1\alpha_2 \qquad :0$$
$$\alpha_1 \rightarrow \cdot\, \beta_1\beta_2 \qquad :0$$
$$\beta_1 \rightarrow \cdot\, X_1X_2 \qquad :0$$

are in S_0. These correspond to the right-hand chains in the skeleton and can be represented graphically by the dots shown in Figure 8.3. The large dots, corresponding to the dots in the states, indicate a path from σ' to the terminal string. The *bottom* of the path of dots indicates the next terminal symbol to look for.

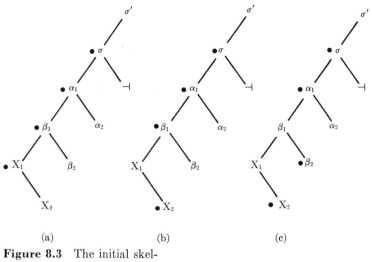

(a)   (b)   (c)

Figure 8.3   The initial skeleton of a translation tree

Suppose now that the next symbol read is, indeed, X_1.   The new state set, S_1, contains [see Figure 8.3(b)]

$$\beta_1 \rightarrow X_1 \cdot X_2 \qquad :0$$

We already know that every left-hand chain of a translation tree ends with a terminal symbol, and that each terminal symbol can only be in one chain.   Thus each left-hand chain corresponds to one, and only one, terminal symbol.   And, as mentioned above, the state set corresponding to a symbol in the terminal string contains states corresponding to the right-hand chains of all possible skeletons that could connect to the next symbol in the string.

In the example, S_0 contained states corresponding to the skeleton pictured.   In S_1, the size of the next possible skeleton has shrunk, in this case to a single state.   The skeleton derivable at the next point is the terminal symbol itself, that is, X_2.   However, to see that this is not always the case, suppose X_2 matches.   Then we have the situation of Figure 8.3(c).   The next skeleton to the terminal string starting at X_3 has as its root β_2, and there may be any number of states corresponding to a left-hand chain from β_2 to X_3.

Since the state set S_0 contains information · about *all possible* skeletons and the procedure carries forward that information in parallel for all possible trees, it can be seen that the procedure actually constructs all possible translation trees and carries them forward only as they are proved to fit the terminal string.   Thus, at the end of the procedure, all legal translation trees will still be indicated in the state set, but only legal trees will remain.

One way of looking at the left-right parse, then, is as a top-down parse that looks at all possible trees at once, and discards them when they prove unfit as the scanning moves from left to right across the input string. The state sets remain at manageable size because of this elimination of alternatives, and because the right-hand chains in the skeletons are entered only once, no matter how often they occur in the skeleton, or, in fact, in how many skeletons they occur.

8.8   reconstructing the translation tree

The algorithm in Section 8.7 is incomplete in the sense of translation. If the last state set contains only the state

$$\sigma \rightarrow \alpha \cdot \qquad :0$$

we know that a legal tree can be built. The sentence has been *recognized*. But what is the tree? It looks like we do not have that information. However, the tree has been generated since the information describing it is implicit in the state sets.

To make unraveling the tree simpler, two data links will be added to the state representation. In a sense these links are redundant information since they reproduce information already available, but they have the advantage of making the tree structure in the state sets explicit rather than implicit. When a state is brought forward, either by indirect or direct generation, a *Prelink* element pointing to its previous form in some earlier state is established. When a state is brought forward by indirect generation, we establish a *Descentlink* pointing to the other state whose completion caused the new state to be entered in the set.

The links can be shown to be redundant. No states that have been generated either directly or indirectly have the dot on the far left since both rules require moving the dot to the right one step. But all states generated by closure have the dot on the extreme left. So the two classes of states can be separated. Now states that were generated by the indirect rule have the dot immediately to the right of a variable symbol. This observation follows directly from the generation rules.

Suppose there is a state

$$\beta \rightarrow \bar{x}\gamma \cdot \bar{y} \qquad :i \qquad (8.1)$$

in a state set, S_j.   By the previous observation, it was brought forward by the indirect rule.   This means that a state with γ as root must be in S_j, and that state must have the dot at the far right-hand side of it. It appears as

$$\gamma \to \bar{z} \cdot \qquad : \mathrm{k} \qquad\qquad (8.2)$$

If this state was initiated by the phrase represented by (8.1), state set S_k must contain the state

$$\beta \to \bar{x} \cdot \gamma\bar{y} \qquad : \mathrm{i} \qquad\qquad (8.3)$$

If S_k contains this state, (8.2) is a descendant of (8.1) since it caused the latter to be brought forward in an indirect generation.   Thus *Descentlink* is known.   In this case, *Prelink* is also known; it is the state (8.3) in S_k.

If the state is

$$\beta \to \bar{x}A \cdot \bar{y} \qquad : \mathrm{i}$$

Descentlink is not needed, and *Prelink* is merely the state

$$\beta \to \bar{x} \cdot A\bar{y} \qquad : \mathrm{i}$$

in the immediate preceding state set, S_{j-1}.

These links describe the binary tree directly, although backward. The *Prelink*s connect the chain associated with a production, but

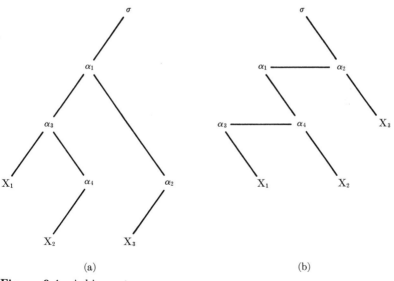

(a)   (b)

Figure 8.4 A binary translation tree (a) and its backward form (b)

from left to right.   The *Descentlink*s point to the rightmost element of a phrase descendant from a variable.   The links form a backward binary tree that is merely another form of the translation tree.   Thus, for example, instead of Figure 8.4(a), we have 8.4(b), where *Prelink*s form the right-hand chain and *Descentlink*s form the left-hand chain.

8.9   an example

Let us set up as an example a simple grammar for arithmetic expressions using a single operand A, and only the $+$ and $\times$ operations along with parentheses.   The original grammar is defined below.

$$G = (\{A, +, \times, (,)\}, \{\alpha, \beta, \gamma\}, \Pi, \alpha)$$
$$\Pi = \{\alpha \to \alpha + \beta \qquad :1$$
$$\dot{\alpha} \to \beta \qquad :2$$
$$\beta \to \beta \times \gamma \qquad :3$$
$$\beta \to \gamma \qquad :4$$
$$\gamma \to A \qquad :5$$
$$\gamma \to (\alpha) \qquad :6\}$$

It must first be modified as follows.

$$G' = (\{A, +, \times, (,), \dashv\}, \{\sigma, \alpha, \beta, \gamma\}, \Pi', \sigma)$$
$$\Pi' = \{\sigma \to \alpha\dashv \qquad :1$$
$$\alpha \to \alpha + \beta \qquad :2$$
$$\alpha \to \beta \qquad :3$$
$$\beta \to \beta \times \gamma \qquad :4$$
$$\beta \to \gamma \qquad :5$$
$$\gamma \to A \qquad :6$$
$$\gamma \to (\alpha) \qquad :7\}$$

Before the input string is even approached, S_0 can be constructed. It is the same for G' over all possible inputs.   To start with,

$$S_0 = \{\sigma \to \cdot\, \alpha\dashv \qquad :0\}$$

Now apply closure on α.

$$S_0 = \{\sigma \to \cdot\, \alpha\dashv \qquad :0$$
$$\alpha \to \cdot\, \alpha + \beta \qquad :0$$
$$\alpha \to \cdot\, \beta \qquad :0\}$$

A new variable, β, has appeared directly to the right of a dot, so again apply closure, this time on β.

$$S_0 = \{\sigma \rightarrow \cdot \, \alpha \dashv \qquad :0$$
$$\alpha \rightarrow \cdot \, \alpha + \beta \qquad :0$$
$$\alpha \rightarrow \cdot \, \beta \qquad :0$$
$$\beta \rightarrow \cdot \, \beta \times \gamma \qquad :0$$
$$\beta \rightarrow \cdot \, \gamma \qquad :0\}$$

There is still another variable, γ.   Again apply closure.

$$S_0 = \{\sigma \rightarrow \cdot \, \alpha \dashv \qquad :0$$
$$\alpha \rightarrow \cdot \, \alpha + \beta \qquad :0$$
$$\alpha \rightarrow \cdot \, \beta \qquad :0$$
$$\beta \rightarrow \cdot \, \beta \times \gamma \qquad :0$$
$$\beta \rightarrow \cdot \, \gamma \qquad :0$$
$$\gamma \rightarrow \cdot \, A \qquad :0$$
$$\gamma \rightarrow \cdot \, (\alpha) \qquad :0\}$$

There are no new terminal symbols to worry about, so the initial state set is finished.   In fact, for this case, all productions in the grammar are represented in S_0, so we have to be finished.

Now take a simple input string, label each symbol, and remember to terminate the string with a $\dashv$.

$$\begin{array}{cccccc} A & + & A & \times & A & \dashv \\ 1 & 2 & 3 & 4 & 5 & 6 \end{array}$$

Let us build state sets for each point.   First, to build S_1, apply the direct rule to S_0 to get

$$\gamma \rightarrow A \cdot \qquad :0$$

as the first state added to S_1.   There are no more direct constructions possible.   How about the indirect rule?

The state now in S_1 has a dot at the end of its right-hand side, so the indirect rule can be applied.   Go to S_0 (the starting point for that state) and bring up any states that have a dot immediately to the left of a γ, since a γ has been found.   The following states are now in S_1:

$$S_1 = \{\gamma \rightarrow A \cdot \qquad :0$$
$$\beta \rightarrow \gamma \cdot \qquad :0\}$$

Now apply the indirect rule repeatedly,

$$S_1 = \{\gamma \to A \cdot \qquad\qquad :0$$
$$\beta \to \gamma \cdot \qquad\qquad :0$$
$$\beta \to \beta \cdot \times \gamma \qquad :0$$
$$\alpha \to \beta \cdot \qquad\qquad :0$$
$$\alpha \to \alpha \cdot + \beta \qquad :0$$
$$\sigma \to \alpha \cdot \dashv \qquad\qquad :0\}$$

No more indirect transfers can be made, and the closure rule gives no additional terms.

Now S_2 is built by first reading the $+$. Applying the direct rule followed by closure yields

$$S_2 = \{\alpha \to \alpha + \cdot \beta \qquad :0$$
$$\beta \to \cdot \beta \times \gamma \qquad :2$$
$$\beta \to \cdot \gamma \qquad\qquad :2$$
$$\gamma \to \cdot A \qquad\qquad :2$$
$$\gamma \to \cdot (\alpha) \qquad\qquad :2\}$$

In other words, all of the hypothetical skeletons rooted at σ have been eliminated from consideration but one, the one shown in Figure 8.5.

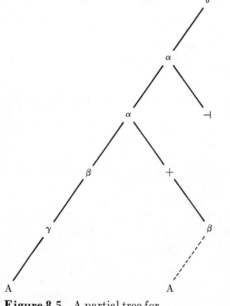

Figure 8.5   A partial tree for
sample parse

The processor now needs to search for a tree from β to the part of the remaining string starting at A, the third symbol of the input. The state set S_3 is then constructed as the following.

$$S_3 = \{\gamma \rightarrow A \cdot \qquad\qquad :2$$
$$\beta \rightarrow \gamma \cdot \qquad\qquad :2$$
$$\beta \rightarrow \beta \cdot \times \gamma \qquad :2\}$$

Continuing, read the $\times$ symbol and construct S_4.

$$S_4 = \{\beta \rightarrow \beta \times \cdot \gamma \qquad :2$$
$$\gamma \rightarrow \cdot A \qquad\qquad :4$$
$$\gamma \rightarrow \cdot (\alpha) \qquad\qquad :4\}$$

Then do the same for S_5.

$$S_5 = \{\gamma \rightarrow A \cdot \qquad\qquad :4$$
$$\beta \rightarrow \beta \times \gamma \cdot \qquad :2$$
$$\beta \rightarrow \beta \cdot \times \gamma \qquad :2$$
$$\alpha \rightarrow \alpha + \beta \cdot \qquad :0$$
$$\alpha \rightarrow \alpha \cdot + \beta \qquad :0$$
$$\alpha \rightarrow \alpha \cdot \dashv \qquad\qquad :0\}$$

This set deserves some attention. The second state in S_5 is obtained indirectly from S_4, since that is where the completed state started looking for a γ. The next states are derived indirectly from the second state in S_5, but are obtained from S_2. In fact, both the second and third states in S_5 derive originally from the same state in S_2, an illustration of how left recursion is taken care of automatically in this procedure. The last two states come from S_0 indirectly due to the completion of the fourth state in S_5.

Finally, generate S_6, associated with the $\dashv$. The direct rule applies, and that is all. So we obtain

$$S_6 = \{\sigma \rightarrow \alpha \dashv \cdot \qquad :0\}$$

Thus the form of the final state set is the necessary condition for recognition, and the sentence has been recognized. The illustration of the state sets, Figure 8.6, indicates the *Descentlinks* and the *Prelinks* that could have been generated either during the translation or afterward. For clarity of displays, the order of states in the sets has been shifted from those above, and only those links involved with the final translation tree are shown. Figure 8.7 shows the reverse binary tree structured in the state sets.

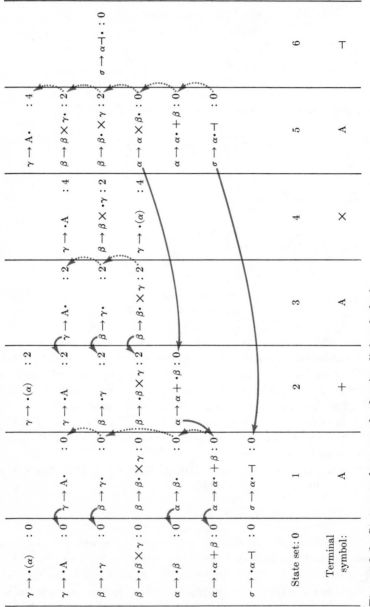

Figure 8.6 State sets for example showing links; dashed arrows are *Prelinks*, solid arrows are *Descentlinks*

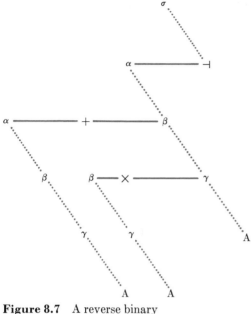

Figure 8.7   A reverse binary
tree from example

8.10   *characteristics of the algorithm*

The left-right algorithm has been studied in some detail by J. Earley
[11]. He has shown that, as a translator of general context-free
languages, it outperforms the purely top-down and bottom-up parsing
algorithms.

   The algorithm's time bound for translation is proportional to
m^3, where m is the length of the input string. If the input string
is doubled in length, the translator will take at most eight times
as much time. This time seems long, but considering the considerable
amount of backtracking required by the other two algorithms for
some grammars, the bound looks pretty good. In fact, the time
bounds for these other grammars are exponential. That is, they are
proportional to C^m, where C is some constant and m is the length
of the string.

   In addition to the above bound, Earley also shows that the bound
is proportional to m^2 for unambiguous grammars, and even shrinks
to proportional to m for a large subset of unambiguous grammars.
These results are somewhat surprising since the algorithm is more
general than most. It generates all translation trees of an unambig-

uous sentence, allows left recursion, and can even handle ε-producing grammars.

Of course, bounds are tricky. Although they are important results, they do not prove one technique *is* faster than another. They only indicate the best that can be said about each technique. In arithmetic, for example, the set of inequalities $9 > x$ and $7 > y$ does *not* imply that $x > y$. However, experiments on specific sentences of some grammars indicate that, for those experiments at least, the left-right algorithm is as fast or faster than top-down or bottom-up techniques.

problems

In the first two problems, use the following grammar.

$$G = (\Sigma,\ T,\ \Pi,\ \sigma)$$

where

$$
\begin{aligned}
\Pi = \{ &\sigma \to \alpha & :1 \\
&\alpha \to AB\delta & :2 \\
&\alpha \to C & :3 \\
&\delta \to AB & :4 \\
&\delta \to \beta\alpha D & :5 \\
&\beta \to \alpha B & :6\}
\end{aligned}
$$

1. Construct the closure of the following partial state sets.

(a) $S_i = \{ \delta \to \beta \cdot \alpha \qquad :3$
$\phantom{S_i = \{} \delta \to AB \cdot \qquad :4\}$

(b) $S_i = \{\alpha \to AB \cdot \delta \qquad :3\}$

(c) $S_i = \{\alpha \to A \cdot B \qquad :4$
$\phantom{S_i = \{} \beta \to \alpha \cdot B \qquad :2$
$\phantom{S_i = \{} \delta \to A \cdot B \qquad :4\}$

2. Given the following partial state sets

S_1		S_2		S_3		S_4
$\sigma \to \cdot\, \alpha$	:0	$\beta \to \cdot\, B\beta$	:2	$\beta \to B \cdot \beta$	:2	
$\alpha \to \cdot\, \beta A$	:1	$\beta \to B \cdot$	:1	$\beta \to \cdot\, \beta$	:3	
$\beta \to \cdot\, B\beta$	:1	$\alpha \to \beta \cdot A$	:1	$\beta \to B \cdot$	:2	
$\beta \to \cdot\, B$	:1			$\beta \to B\beta \cdot$	:2	
				$\alpha \to \beta \cdot A$	:1	

$X_1 = B$ $\qquad\qquad$ $X_2 = B$ $\qquad\qquad$ $X_3 = B$ $\qquad\qquad$ $X_4 = A$

(a) Apply the direct generation rule to find states for S_4.

(b) Apply the indirect rule to find additional states for S_4.

(c) Apply the closure rule to S_4.

3. Show that the state

$$\sigma' \rightarrow \cdot \sigma \dashv \qquad :i$$

can only occur in S_0, and thus that i = 0.

4. Show that, given any skeleton on a translation tree derivable from σ', every right-hand chain in it is represented in the state set S_0.

5. Given an input string of length n ≥ i, show that the direct rule applied to S_{i-1} fails to bring any states into S_i, if and only if there are no legal translation trees for the input string.

6. Given the grammar for simple arithmetic expressions presented in Section 8.9, apply the parallel parse to the following expressions.

(a) A × (A + B)
(b) A + A + A

7. Show the reverse binary trees and the normal binary translation trees for the above examples.

8. Develop the preorder walks of all four of the above trees and compare them.

9. Develop an algorithm that, using the links in the state sets and starting at the final entry, will output the preorder walk of the binary translation tree.

10. Implement the left-right parse.

9

restricted grammars

There is a great deal of trial and error processing and backtracking when parsing a sentence in a general context-free language by using the three algorithms discussed in the previous chapters. The root of the problem is that a phrase can never be recognized for certain until the final terminal symbol in the input string has been recognized and a possible translation tree built.

Let us look at an example of this problem, using a very simple language that, nevertheless, drives most general context-free translation algorithms mad.

$$G = (\{A\}, \{\alpha\}, \{\alpha \rightarrow A, \alpha \rightarrow A\alpha A\}, \alpha)$$

The language consists of all odd-length strings of the symbol A.

$$\Lambda(G) = \{A^{n+1} \mid n = 0, 1, 2, \ldots\}$$

Now each A in the string is a candidate for being the handle, although only one actually is a prime phrase. Suppose the string is n characters long. Then the A at position $(n + 1)/2$ is the handle. But, since location of the handle depends on n, the translation routine must know the length of the string before it correctly assigns this phrase. To know the length of the string, the processor must read the whole input, hypothesizing at each step (wrongly, except at the end) about the location of the handle.

There appears to be a serious limit to the speed and efficiency of translators for context-free languages, caused by the need to account for a wide variety of syntactic behavior. But many useful languages do not require the breadth of definition inherent in the context-free formulation. Narrower, more restrictive classes of languages can be defined that can be handled by more efficient translation techniques. These techniques limit and sometimes completely eliminate backtracking by providing tests that allow the translator to predict with some degree of certainty whether a candidate for the handle of a sentential form is the handle or not, without having to develop the actual tree. This and the following chapters will discuss some of the special classes of languages that have been defined and their translation algorithms.

To start our exploration of improving the parsing of sentences, let us look first at a modification of the left-right algorithm discussed in Chapter 8.

9.1   prediction in the parallel parse

Suppose that, for each production in a grammar, we could obtain a list of terminal symbols $(K_1, K_2, \ldots, K_n)$ that contains all of the terminal symbols that could possibly follow immediately to the right of the phrase generated by that production in a sentence. This set will be called the *right context set* of the production. For example, in the simple arithmetic-expression language presented in Chapter 8, look at the production

$$\delta \rightarrow (\alpha)$$

This production defines another operand in an expression, this operand being another expression surrounded by parentheses. But an operand must be followed by either an operator, right parenthesis, or the end-of-string symbol $\dashv$. It cannot be followed by another operand or a left parenthesis. (Our grammar has not incorporated the concept of *implicit multiplication*, in which two operands written together means that they are to be multiplied.) Thus the right context set of the production is $\{+, \times,), \dashv\}$.

Now suppose that we are proceeding along with a parallel parse, and that the state

$$\delta \rightarrow (\alpha)\cdot \qquad :k$$

is added to some state set $S_i(i > k)$. Now the indirect generation rule says that the translator has found an occurrence of a phrase rooted at δ and terminating at the symbol X_i, and thus the state in S_k that called for the search for this phrase should be carried forward. But now the right context set for the production is known. Why not peek at X_{i+1} and see if it is an allowable next symbol? If not, we know right away that the phrase is not valid in any legal translation tree for that sentence, for, if it were possible, X_{i+1} would have to be in the right context set, by definition.

That is, in mathematical terms, membership of X_{i+1} in the right context set of the production is *necessary but not sufficient* for the production to be in a legal translation tree. So there is a way to eliminate some but not all false trails early by imposing a test before a state is carried forward in the indirect generation.

Thus the definition of state is modified by defining a state to be an ordered quadruplet of elements consisting of a production; a location in the production (the dot); an index to a previous state set; and a new entry, the right context set for that production. The indirect generation rule is modified by preceding its carrying forward the previous state by a test to see whether the next symbol to be scanned is in its right context set. If it is, the indirect generation is carried through. If it is not, the rule is not applied to this state. Whether this modification saves time and effort for the translator depends, of course, on the particular grammar. But since the algorithm is for the general class of context-free languages and there are grammars for which translation would be significantly improved, it can be said that the change causes an overall improvement.

The modification can be generalized. Suppose that, instead of just one-symbol contexts, strings of length 2, 3, or, in general, k termination symbols, are associated with each production set as the legal right contexts. These sets are called the *k-right contexts* of the production. The translator uses these expanded contexts to compare the next k terminal symbols in the input string to the right of X_i with the k-right context set of the finished state before applying the indirect generation rule to put a state in S_i. As k grows, the test gets stronger and stronger (though not necessarily decisive at any point) and the ability to weed out unqualified partial trees early in the process improves. But, of course, a penalty is paid. The state stored gets bigger and bigger as k increases. In fact, the bound on the number of possible symbols in the k-right context set is kn^k where n is the number of terminal symbols in the grammar. The test for matching strings of length k grows similarly time-consuming. It seems clear that the additional effort required for the algorithm as k grows may soon become greater than it is worth in terms of translation efficiency.

9.2   calculation of right contexts

The procedure described in Section 9.1 requires the calculation of k-right context sets for all productions in a grammar G.   An algorithm will be developed here for this calculation, first for the case of k = 1, then for the general case.   This type of calculation, or some form of it, is used in the translation algorithm for some of the other classes of grammars presented later, so its importance is not limited to the predictive parse discussed above.

To find the k-right context set of any production

$$\alpha \rightarrow \bar{x}$$

we want to know what possible strings of terminal characters can lie to the right of the phrase $\bar{x}$, or to the right of the appearance of α in a sentential form.   First, define for each variable α, a *left terminal set*, consisting of all terminal symbols that can be on the left end of a phrase rooted at α.   Call this set $L(\alpha)$.   Now, add to $L(\alpha)$ all terminal symbols that appear directly on the left-hand end of productions with α as the root.   That is, if

$$\alpha \rightarrow x_1 x_2 \cdot \cdot \cdot x_n$$

is a valid production and if the element x_1 is a terminal symbol, we know that a terminal phrase produced by α can possibly start with x_1.

Suppose that x_1 is a variable.   Then

$$L(\alpha) \supset L(x_1)$$

for any symbol in $L(x_1)$ must also be a left-hand terminal for a phrase produced by α.

This argument suggests an algorithm for constructing a sequence of sets $L_i(\alpha)$ that will provide us with the left terminal sets.

Algorithm: Left-Set

Left-Set 1:   For each variable ξ, construct an $L_0(\xi)$ as follows:

$$L_0(\xi) = \{A \mid \xi \rightarrow A\bar{x} \text{ is a production in } \Pi\}$$

Left-Set 2:   Given a set of $L_i(\alpha)$ for all $\alpha \in$ T, construct $L_{i+1}(\xi)$ as follows:

$$L_{i+1}(\xi) = L_i(\xi) \cup \{A \mid \xi \to \alpha\bar{x} \text{ and } A \in L_i(\alpha)\}$$

Basically, the algorithm constructs improving approximations to the left terminal sets. The first approximation of $L(\alpha)$ is all terminal symbols appearing on the left of arguments having α as the root. This set is $L_0(\alpha)$. Refinements are made by including left-terminal-set approximations for variables appearing on the left of arguments having α as their root.

This process is continued for increasing i until no new symbols are being added to the sets, that is, $L_{i+1}(\xi) = L_i(\xi)$ for all ξ in T. That, of course, must happen since there are a finite number of sets, one for each variable, and a finite number of terminal symbols they can contain. It is not hard to show that once the procedure stops generating new members of the sets, it stops for good (see Problem 1). Say that the process stops adding elements at $L_k(\xi)$. That is,

$$L_k(\xi) = L_{k+1}(\xi) = L_{k+2}(\xi) \cdots \qquad \text{for all } \xi$$

The reader will be asked to show that

$$L(\xi) = L_k(\xi)$$

where L is the originally defined left terminal set of ξ.

Now that the left terminal sets of all variables have been found, we can generate the 1-right context set of ξ. Suppose ξ occurs in the right-hand side of a production as follows:

$$\alpha \to \bar{x}\xi y\bar{z}$$

where $\bar{x}$ or $y\bar{z}$ may be null.

Case 1:   The symbol y is a terminal symbol. Then y is in the 1-right context set of ξ.

Case 2:   The symbol y is a variable, in which case all the members of the left terminal set of y are 1-right contexts of ξ.

Case 3:   The string $y\bar{z}$ is null. In this case, the 1-right context of ξ contains the 1-right context of α.

Thus the algorithm for calculating the k-right context of the variable ξ is as follows:

Algorithm: 1-Right Context

1-Right C 1:   Calculate the left terminal sets for all variables in the grammar.

1-Right C 2: (Case 1) For all ξ in T, let $RC_0(\xi)$ be the set of all terminal symbols that occur as right-hand neighbors of ξ in the argument of a production in Π.

$$RC_0(\xi) = \{X \mid \text{there is some production}$$

$$\alpha \to \bar{y}\xi X\bar{z} \text{ in } \Pi\}$$

1-Right C 3: (Case 2) For all ξ in T, let $RC_1(\xi)$ be $RC_0(\xi)$ plus the union of left terminal sets of all variables that occur as right-hand neighbors of ξ in arguments of productions in Π.

$$RC_1(\xi) = RC_0(\xi) \cup \{\bigcup_{\beta} \{L(\beta) \mid \alpha \to \bar{y}\xi\beta\bar{z} \text{ in } \Pi\}\}$$

1-Right C 4: (Case 3) For i = 2 until no new entries are added to the old sets, and for each ξ in T, let $RC_i(\xi)$ be $RC_{i-1}(\xi)$ plus $RC_{i-1}(\alpha)$ for all variables α that are roots of productions in which ξ is the rightmost element of the argument.

$$RC_i(\xi) = RC_{i-1}(\xi) \cup \{\bigcup_{\alpha} \{RC_{i-1}(\alpha) \mid \alpha \to \bar{y}\xi \text{ in } \Pi\}$$

9.3   PR(k) grammars

The parallel algorithm was improved by increasing its ability to weed out false leads early, but it is, in general, not possible to say that matching a k-right context with the terminal string guarantees that the phrase recognized is in fact part of a true translation tree. It merely becomes more likely as k grows larger. However, there are particular grammars for which such a guarantee can be made. Let us define such a class.

Definition 9.1: Let G be a grammar, and $\Lambda(G)$ be the language generated by it. The grammar G is said to be PR(k) if, for every sentence in the grammar, every state generated indirectly during the k-modified parse belongs to the final representation of the translation tree.

9.4   analytic and synthetic contexts

In a sentential form, the context of a symbol is the pair of substrings immediately to the left and right of it. But it is necessary to clarify the difference between the concept of context as it pertains to the generation, or synthesis, of strings, and as it pertains to the parsing, or analytical process.

Context has already been used in the terms *context-free* and *context-sensitive* grammars. This type of context, as you recall, refers to the application of substitution rules for syntactic variables when building sentences. This form of context could be called *synthetic context* since it is a property of the synthesis process. Thus a context-free grammar allows a substitution rule to be applied to a variable independent of the string surrounding it. A context-sensitive grammar allows substitutions only when the variable is surrounded by certain specified substrings of symbols. Once the generation has been made by either means the newly substituted phrase has a context that is often used for analysis. There is no inconsistency, then, in talking about context in parsing context-free languages. One important structure of contexts in a sentence is in fact the nesting of sub-phrases in larger phrases.

For example, look at the partial production set below.

$$\{\alpha \to C\nu C \quad :1$$
$$\gamma \to A\beta C \quad :2$$
$$\beta \to B \quad :3$$
$$\nu \to B \quad :4\}$$

These productions are context-free, and they can be imagined embedded in a full context-free grammar. Now suppose the following two substrings are in sentences generated by the grammar.

$$\cdots CBC \cdots$$
$$\cdots ABC \cdots$$

Now, whether the B is produced by production 3 or 4 is ambiguous if it is examined by itself. Which production is proper depends on the larger phrase in which B is embedded. If a C precedes it, production 4 is called for; if an A, production 3. Therefore, even though the productions are context-free in one sense, the context of the symbol B is useful information when translating the sentence. However, the context is not necessary information. In fact, the first three translation algorithms (top-down, bottom-up, and left-right) do not use context information directly. But they are also relatively inefficient techniques. The modified parallel algorithm, on the other hand, uses context information to improve its performance.

Let us now look at what context information is available at any step of this process. Suppose the process is at the i-th input character, X_i. According to the previous discussion of the parallel process, the only states that can be carried into S_i, the corresponding state set, are states corresponding to subtrees in the translation trees that are still possible given the partial input string $X_1X_2 \cdot \cdot \cdot X_i$. That is, since the routine reads from left to right, all characters to the left of X_i have been used as implicit contextual information in trying to build hypothetical translation trees. Suppose, further, that a possible phrase ends at X_{i-1}. As we have seen earlier, this occurrence implies that a state corresponding to this phrase will be carried forward. If a k-modified algorithm is being used, this state will be carried forward if and only if the next k characters match the legal contexts for the phrase.

The PR(k) definition puts together the two contextual processes that determine that a handle has been identified. The subtree is a part of the partial tree built by the left-right algorithm to conform to the left-hand context, and the k right-hand symbols conform to the k-right context of the phrase.

9.5 *LR(k) grammars*

There is a class of languages similar to PR(k) that first appeared in the literature in 1965 in an article by D. E. Knuth [16]. This class, labeled LR(k), forms the least restrictive set of unambiguous grammars known and thus forms a nice extreme point in the spectrum of language classes. It derives from a requirement that it should be possible to tell whether a possible handle is really the handle of the sentence by looking at the full left context and the k-length right context of the possible phrase. The PR(k) grammars are not that general, surprisingly enough, as will be shown later.

First, let us formalize the above definition.

Definition 9.2: Let the string $\bar{s}$ be partitioned as follows:

$$\bar{s} = \bar{u}\bar{v}\bar{w}\bar{x}$$

The following assumptions are made about the partitioned string.

The substring $\bar{u}$ is of arbitrary length and composed of terminal symbols and variables. The substring $\bar{v}$ is the handle of $\bar{s}$. The substring $\bar{w}$ is of length k, and is composed of terminal symbols only as is $\bar{x}$, the remainder of $\bar{s}$.

The production $\alpha \rightarrow \bar{v}$ satisfies the LR(k) condition if and only if it either always forms a handle in the context $\bar{u}\bar{v}\bar{w} \cdot \cdot \cdot$, or never does. That is, if there exists any sentential form,

$$\bar{s}' = \bar{u}\bar{v}\bar{w}\bar{y}$$

in which $\alpha \rightarrow \bar{v}$ forms the handle, then it forms the handle of s̄. A grammar is an LR(k) grammar if and only if its productions all satisfy the LR(k) condition.

To illustrate, look at a grammar that is not LR(k).

$$G_1 = (\{A\}, \{\alpha\}, \Pi, \alpha)$$

where

$$\Pi = \{\alpha \rightarrow A\alpha A \quad :1$$
$$\alpha \rightarrow A \quad :2\}$$

It is a grammar we have seen before, which produces the set of all finite, odd-length strings of A's. The handle of the sentence in the language is the middle A, to which production 2 is applied. But, how does the processor know it is at the middle unless it has counted the elements of the string, and how can it count them without reading the entire string? If the string has $2k + 1$ A's or more, it is undecidable whether the handle is, in fact, the handle from looking only k terms to the right. The string appears as follows:

$$\text{A} \cdots \text{A} \quad \text{A} \quad \text{A} \cdots \text{A} \quad \dashv$$
$$1 \cdots k \quad k+1 \quad k+2 \quad 2k+1 \quad 2k+2$$

Now, is element $k + 1$ the handle or not? Of course it is, but the translator would know that only by looking at the $(k + 1)$th right-hand-side element and identifying it as a $\dashv$ rather than an A. Since for any k you could supply, I can construct a sentence that requires the translator to look $k + 1$ characters to the right to decide on the handle, then the grammar is not LR(k). The k must be fixed for the entire language. Incidentally, this example also shows that the set of LR(k) grammars does not include *all* unambiguous grammars.

You are going to be asked to show that unambiguous PR(k) grammars are LR(k). To show that unambiguous PR(k) grammars are a *proper* subset of LR(k), that is, that there exist LR(k) grammars that are not PR(k), examine the following grammar.

$$G_2 = (\{A, B, C, D, E\}, \{\alpha, \beta, \gamma\}, \Pi, \alpha)$$
$$\Pi = \{\alpha \rightarrow A\gamma \quad :1$$
$$\alpha \rightarrow A\beta C \quad :2$$
$$\alpha \rightarrow E\beta D \quad :3$$
$$\beta \rightarrow B \quad :4$$
$$\gamma \rightarrow BD \quad :5\}$$
$$\Lambda(G_2) = \{ABD, ABC, EBD\}$$

To see why G_2 is not PR(k), let us parse ABD. The translation tree is shown in Figure 9.1(a). When state set S_2 is constructed,

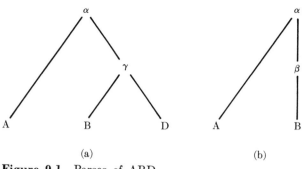

(a)   (b)

Figure 9.1 Parses of ABD

corresponding to the second symbol, B, a possible partial tree results, as shown in Figure 9.1(b). Now, before putting the state

$$\beta \to B \cdot \quad : 1$$

in S_2, the processor looks at the next symbol, the right context. It is a D. But D is certainly a legitimate right context for the production 4 (in the sentence EBD), so the state is accepted wrongly. It would not help to look further by using a larger k. So the grammar is not PR(k) for any k. On the other hand, the grammar is clearly LR(1).

What went wrong? The answer is that the contexts are taken independently in the PR(k) definition, and together in the LR(k) definition. That is, the string A is a valid left context for production 4 in the sentence ABC. And D is a perfectly acceptable right context for the same production in the sentence EBD. But the total context (A,D) taken together is *not* a valid context pair, as the LR(k) definition requires. The left-right algorithm can be modified to test for LR(k) by recalculating the possible right contexts for a production when constructing the state set, using only the possible partial trees constructed to that point, rather than using the entire grammar and calculating the complete set of possible k-right contexts before parsing begins.

problems

1. Show that, if $L_i(\xi) = L_{i+1}(\xi)$ for all ξ in T for some i, then $L_i(\xi) = L_{i+1}(\xi)$ for all k > 1.

2. (a) Show that $L_0(\xi)$ is the set of *all* terminals reached from the node ξ by a left-hand chain of length 1.

   (b) Show that, if $L_i(\xi)$ is the set of all terminals reached from ξ by a left-hand chain of length $\leq i + 1$, then $L_{i+1}(\xi)$ is the set of all terminals reached from ξ by a left-hand chain of length $\leq i + 2$.

   (c) It was shown in Chapter 5 that there was a maximum length for nonrecursive left-hand chains. Call this maximum k. Show that $L_k(\xi) = L(\xi)$. Why can the recursive chains be ignored?

3. (a) Let $\Psi^k(\xi)$ be defined as the set of terminal-symbol substrings of length k that can be at the extreme left of a phrase generated by the node ξ. That is,

   $$\Psi^k(\xi) = \{\bar{x} \mid \xi \overset{*}{\Rightarrow} \bar{x}\bar{y},\ |\bar{x}| = k, \text{ and } \bar{x} \in \Sigma^*\}$$

   Develop an algorithm to calculate these k-left terminal substrings.

   (b) Let $\Phi^k(\xi)$ be defined as the set of terminal *phrases* of length less than k generated by ξ. That is,

   $$\Phi^k(\xi) = \{\bar{x} \mid \xi \overset{*}{\Rightarrow} \bar{x},\ |\bar{x}| < k, \text{ and } \bar{x} \in \Sigma\}$$

   Assuming we have a $\Psi^k(\xi)$ and $\Phi^k(\xi)$ for each variable ξ in the grammar, use them to construct the k-right contexts of all variables in the grammar.

4. Show that the following grammar is LR(1)

   $$G = (\{A, B\}, \{a\}, \Pi, \alpha)$$

   where

   $$\Pi = \{\alpha \to A\alpha B \quad :1$$
   $$\phantom{\Pi = \{}\alpha \to A \quad\quad\ :2\}$$

5. Show that an unambiguous PR(k) grammar is LR(k).

6. Show that grammar G_2 is LR(1).

7. Are the following grammars PR(k), LR(k), or neither? What is the value of k, if it exists?

   (a) $G = (\{A\}, \{a\}, \Pi, \alpha)$
   $$\Pi = \{\alpha \to \alpha AA \quad :1$$
   $$\phantom{\Pi = \{}\alpha \to A \quad\quad\ :2\}$$

(b) (Knuth) $G = (\{A, B, C\}, \{\sigma, \alpha\}, \Pi, \sigma)$

$\Pi = \{\sigma \rightarrow A\alpha C \qquad :1$

$\qquad \sigma \rightarrow B \qquad\qquad :2$

$\qquad \alpha \rightarrow A\sigma C \qquad :3$

$\qquad \alpha \rightarrow B \qquad\qquad :4\}$

(c) (Knuth) $G = (\{A, B, C, D\}, \{\sigma, \alpha, \beta\}, \Pi, \sigma)$

$\Pi = \{\sigma \rightarrow A\alpha D \qquad :1$

$\qquad \sigma \rightarrow B\alpha\beta \qquad :2$

$\qquad \alpha \rightarrow C\alpha \qquad\quad :3$

$\qquad \alpha \rightarrow C \qquad\qquad :4$

$\qquad \beta \rightarrow D \qquad\qquad :5\}$

(d) $G = (\{A, B, C, D\}, \{\sigma, \alpha, \beta\}, \Pi, \sigma)$

$\Pi = \{\sigma \rightarrow A\alpha D \qquad :1$

$\qquad \sigma \rightarrow A\beta C \qquad :2$

$\qquad \alpha \rightarrow B\alpha \qquad\quad :3$

$\qquad \alpha \rightarrow B \qquad\qquad :4$

$\qquad \beta \rightarrow \beta B \qquad\quad :5$

$\qquad \beta \rightarrow B \qquad\qquad :6\}$

10
bounded-context grammars

In Chapter **9** the idea of restricting a grammar to make the parsing more efficient was introduced. The PR(k) and LR(k) restrictions allow the processor to tell when a candidate for the handle of a string is, in fact, the handle. These restricted grammars can be called *phrase oriented*. But the restrictions only eliminate backtracking from the bottom-up parse.

While the LR(k) and PR(k) restrictions will reduce backtracking in the top-down parse and extra effort in the left-right translator, they will not necessarily eliminate them. For example, suppose that there is a partial binary tree developed up to point T_3 in Figure 10.1 and that the generating grammar is LR(k). Now suppose it is not possible to connect α_4 with symbol T_4. What has the LR(k) condition told us in this case? It does not say that there is no other tree; and the processor must backtrack to look for one. There is, however, some information available. Part of the tree can be retained. The subtrees in Figure 10.2(a) and (b), since they are completed, accepted phrases, must exist in any other possible translation tree. So, for example, the next candidate for a tree might be the one shown in Figure 10.2(c). Thus the LR(k) and PR(k) condition cannot eliminate backtracking from a top-down algorithm, although it may simplify it greatly.

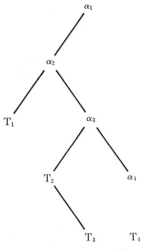

Figure 10.1   A partial translation tree

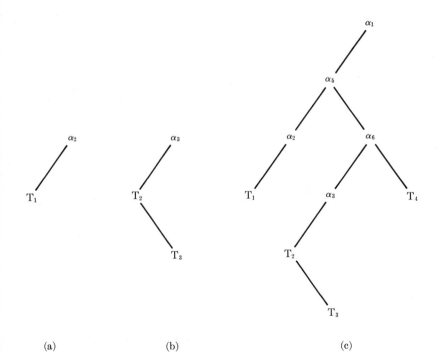

(a)   (b)   (c)

Figure 10.2   Further modifications of the sample tree

10.1   the bottom-up parse and context

The bottom-up parsing algorithm works by searching a string for its handle and substituting the left-hand side of the possible production for that handle. A step in the bottom-up parse applied to a sentential form s is shown schematically below.

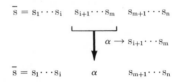

The production $\alpha \to s_{i+1} \cdot \cdot \cdot s_m$ is in the production set for the grammar, and thus the right-hand side, when it occurs in $\bar{s}$, is possibly the handle of the string.

Now, there are two sources of trouble in this step that may cause the translator to backtrack at a later date and discard the step illustrated above.

1. The substring $s_{i+1} \cdot \cdot \cdot s_m$ is the handle, but there is some other production in the grammar with it as the right-hand side. That is, there is a $\beta \to s_{i+1} \cdot \cdot \cdot s_m$ in the grammar where $\beta \neq \alpha$.
2. The substring is not the handle of the string.

In the LR(k) grammar, a limitation was suggested so that the translator would only have to look k symbols to the right and at the entire left substring to determine whether a production did, in fact, generate the handle of the string. If the contexts match a list of possible LR(k) contexts for the production $\alpha \to s_{i+1} \cdot \cdot \cdot s_m$, we are guaranteed that the step illustrated above is correct and that no backtracking is necessary.

But what is the maximum size of i? Is there a maximum size, in fact? After all, the lengths of the left-hand contexts of a handle can be unbounded as can be seen from the very simple example below.

$$G = (\{A, B\}, \{\alpha\}, \Pi, \alpha)$$

where

$$\Pi = \{\alpha \to A\alpha \quad :1$$
$$\alpha \to AB \quad :2\}$$
$$\Lambda(G) = \{A^m B \mid m \geq 2\}$$

Now, for any sentence in $\Lambda(G)$, say $A^m B$, the handle is AB, so there are $m - 1$ A's preceding the handle. Since m is arbitrary, depending on the sentence, the length of the left context is unbounded.

At first glance we might conclude that, since the number of possible left contexts is infinite, and it would be impossible to list them all with productions 1 or 2, an implementation of an LR(k) translation is impossible. Actually, it has been shown by Knuth that, given an LR(k) grammar, it is possible to construct a procedure to recognize the left-hand contexts of handles in a finite number of steps. The proof will not be presented here, but it relates to the fact that the number of possible nonperiodic skeletons from the starting variable is finite, as was shown in Chapter 4. However, despite the assurances that such a procedure is possible, we cannot say in general how finite a "finite number of steps" is. Thus there are possible practical difficulties in constructing an LR(k) translator to handle arbitrarily defined grammars, in that there is no assurance beforehand that the procedure will even fit the computer. However, given a specific grammar already defined, it could be possible to build an efficient LR(k) translator for it.

10.2   right bounded context

Look at the example below, which is similar to, but slightly more elaborate than, the one in the previous section.

$$G = (\{A, B, C\}, \{\alpha, \beta, \delta\}, \Pi, \alpha)$$

where

$$\Pi = \{\alpha \to \delta \qquad :1$$
$$\alpha \to \beta \qquad :2$$
$$\delta \to C\delta \qquad :3$$
$$\beta \to A\beta \qquad :4$$
$$\delta \to B \qquad :5$$
$$\beta \to B \qquad :6\}$$

$$\Lambda(G) = \{C^n B, A^n B \mid n \geq 1\}$$

The handle of any sentence in Λ is the final symbol, the B. A binary translation tree for the sentence appears in Figure 10.3. In the tree, B is the first substring that can be reduced to a variable, in this case δ.

Now suppose that the translator does read a B in translating a sentence in Λ. This substring could be produced by either production 5 or 6. Which is used? The answer, of course, depends on the context. If the symbol directly to the left of the B is C, the tree consists of the δ series of productions; if the symbol to the left is an A, the β series is being used. Now look at the translation

Figure 10.3   A tree for CCCB

process at a later stage. Suppose there is the sentential form CCδ, already reduced from the sample sentence. There are two possible handles in this string terminating with the δ.

$$\alpha \to \delta \qquad :1$$
or $$\delta \to C\delta \qquad :3$$

Looking at the possibility of production 1 generating the handle δ, we see that since there is no production with α in the argument, this production must always be used last. There cannot be any string left over other than α when it is applied. One step to the left of δ is the symbol C, and so production 1 cannot generate the handle of the sentential form. However, production 3 *always* applies when Cδ exists in the form.

The above example demonstrates a language that, looked at as LR(k), seems to present complexity since it has an infinite number of left contexts for a handle. Yet, on looking closer, it has much stronger properties than first imagined. In fact, it is possible to tell whether a substring is a handle or not by looking, at most, only one character to the left of the substring; and no characters to the right take part in the decision. The context used to examine for determining the eligibility of a handle is bounded on both sides.

A grammar with this property is called a *right-bounded-context* (j, k) [*or RBC(j, k)*] *grammar*. The word *right* slips into the definition by virtue of the fact that the processor is assumed to be reading the string from left to right and looking for the handle, the leftmost prime phrase. A *left-bounded-context* (j, k) [*LBC(j, k)*] *grammar* could similarly be defined or even, to push to an extreme, a *left-right bounded-context* (j, k) [*LRBC(j, k)*] *grammar* for a translator reading from both sides toward the center.

Now, let us see a more rigorous definition of an RBC(j, k) grammar.

Definition 10.1:   Let $\alpha \rightarrow x_1x_2 \cdots x_n$ be a production in a grammar G. Suppose $\bar{s}$ is a sentential form expressed as follows:

$$\bar{s} = a_1a_2 \cdots a_ib_1b_2 \cdots b_jx_1x_2 \cdots x_nc_1c_2 \cdots c_kd_1d_2 \cdots d_e$$

The production is RBC(j, k) if and only if the existence of any sentential form $\bar{s}'$, generated by G,

$$\bar{s}' = a_1'a_2' \cdots a_i'b_1b_2 \cdots b_jx_1x_2 \cdots x_nc_1c_2 \cdots c_kd_1'd_2' \cdots d_e'$$

in which $\alpha \rightarrow x_1x_2 \cdots x_n$ is the handle implies that $\alpha \rightarrow x_1x_2 \cdots x_n$ is the handle in $\bar{s}$.

Definition 10.2:   If each production in a grammar is RBC(j_i, k_i), then the grammar is *RBC(j', k')* where

$$j' = \max_i j_i \quad \text{and} \quad k' = \max_i k_i$$

If the left-hand string $b_1b_2 \cdots b_j$, and the right-hand string $c_1 \cdots c_k$ occur around $x_1x_2 \cdots x_n$ only and always when it is a handle rooted at α, then $\alpha \rightarrow x_1x_2 \cdots x_n$ is RBC(j, k). Whenever $x_1x_2 \cdots x_n$ appears in a sentential form, it is always surrounded by *some* (j, k) contexts. If the production is RBC(j, k), it is necessary only to ask if that context is one in which $x_1x_2 \cdots x_n$ can be a handle. If so, we know $\alpha \rightarrow x_1x_2 \cdots x_n$ is in the translation tree.

10.3   the RBC algorithm

One version of the RBC algorithm is a simple modification of the bottom-up parse. The procedure looks through the input stream from left to right, at each point looking backward for a possible handle. However, in this algorithm, a set of contexts is stored with each production, which is checked to see if the possible handle is actually one. Since the context checking always assures us one way or the other, we do not need a backtracking routine.

Suppose the grammar is RBC(j, k). Since the algorithm always checks k characters to the right of the input symbol at the top of *Inlist*, some provision has to be made for reading the last k characters for cases in which there are fewer than k symbols to the right in the input string. A similar problem exists in front of *Inlist*. This problem is handled simply by using again the special symbols $\dashv$ and $\vdash$ as end-of-string characters, but this time requiring that, in a language generated by an RBC(j, k) grammar, all sentences are assumed to terminate in k $\dashv$'s and to initiate in j $\vdash$'s. In this way, even the rightmost symbol in the sentential form has k more characters to the right of it and even the leftmost symbol has j characters to the left. This requirement can be taken care of in processing by the initializing routine, but must also be accounted for in the production set when calculating the contexts.

The flow chart for the RBC(j, k) algorithm appears in Figure 10.4. The algorithm is written below, using the same structure and notation as used in Chapter 7, except that the indices are not stored in *Holdstack* since there is no backtracking.

Algorithm: **RBC(j, k)**

RBC 1:   Put j $\vdash$'s in *Holdstack*.

RBC 2:   (Check if done.)   **If** there is more input, **Then Go to** *RBC 3;*
   Else If top of *Holdstack* is the sentence root **Then Exit-**Success;
   Else Exit-Failure;

RBC 3:   **Read** the next input character **Into** *Holdstack*.

RBC 4:   **If** there is no possible handle in *Holdstack* **Then Go to** *RBC 2*.

RBC 5:   (Check the right and left contexts.)   **If** they do not match **Then Go to** *RBC 4;*

RBC 6:   **Output** handle from *Holdstack* **To** *Outlist* along with production index;
   Push root of handle **Onto** *Holdstack;*
   Go to *RBC 4;*

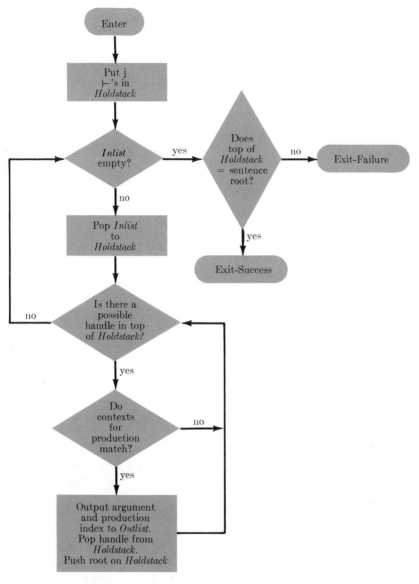

Figure 10.4   RBC(j, k) flow chart

10.4   example of RBC translation

Let us return to our old favorite, the algebraic expression, for an illustration of how the RBC translator works.   The grammar is defined by the production set below, this time in right recursive form.

$$
\begin{aligned}
\Pi = \{ &\langle arithmetic\ expression\rangle \rightarrow \langle term\rangle && :1\\
&\langle arithmetic\ expression\rangle \rightarrow \langle term\rangle\ \langle adding\ operator\rangle\\
&\quad \langle arithmetic\ expression\rangle && :2\\
&\langle term\rangle \rightarrow \langle primary\rangle && :3\\
&\langle term\rangle \rightarrow \langle primary\rangle\ \langle multiplying\ operator\rangle\ \langle term\rangle && :4\\
&\langle primary\rangle \rightarrow (\langle arithmetic\ expression\rangle) && :5\\
&\langle primary\rangle \rightarrow \mathrm{A} && :6\\
&\langle multiplying\ operator\rangle \rightarrow \times && :7\\
&\langle multiplying\ operator\rangle \rightarrow / && :8\\
&\langle adding\ operator\rangle \rightarrow + && :9\\
&\langle adding\ operator\rangle \rightarrow - && :10\}
\end{aligned}
$$

First, see if the grammar is RBC(j, k) and, if it is, assign some values to j and k.   To do so, examine the productions one at a time. First, look at production 10.   The right-hand side is a single terminal symbol, —.   This symbol does not occur in any other production in the set.   Thus, if it is in a sentence, it must have been generated by production 10.   If it is a phrase in the sentence and is encountered on a left-to-right scan, it must be the handle.   No context is involved, and so production 10 is RBC(0, 0).   An identical argument holds for productions 5 to 9, so they are all RBC(0, 0).   While it may be a little more difficult to see, productions 2 and 4 are also RBC(0, 0). The variables $\langle multiplying\ operator\rangle$ and $\langle adding\ operator\rangle$ can be generated in only one way.

Now look at production 3.   Suppose the processor is scanning from left to right and encounters the variable $\langle primary\rangle$, which could be the handle with production 3 as its corresponding production. To decide whether it is, let us ask another question.   How else can $\langle primary\rangle$ be generated? The answer is by production 4. Thus, if $\langle primary\rangle$ is followed by a $\times$ or a $/$, it must be part of a phrase generated by production 4 and so it is not the handle.   However, if $\langle primary\rangle$ is *not* followed by either of the multiplying operators, it must be generated by production 3 and therefore must be the handle. Since we had to look one place to the right and no places to the left to decide whether its argument was the handle, production 3 is RBC(0, 1).   The analysis of production 1 is similar, except that it can be shown to be RBC(1, 1). Since the largest context for a production in the grammar is (1, 1), the grammar is RBC(1, 1).

Now let us work through an example. Some intermediate steps will be left out where they are obvious.

Step	Output (Historical File of Production Indices Only)	Holdstack	Inlist
Initial		⊢	(A + A) × A⊣
(a)		(⊢	A + A) × A⊣
(b)	6	⟨primary⟩ (⊢	+ A) × A⊣

The variable ⟨primary⟩ is a handle if the right-hand context is an operator other than × or /.

| (c) | 6, 3 | ⟨term⟩
 (
 ⊢ | + A) × A⊣ |

Now ⟨term⟩ is a handle if the right-hand context is an operator other than + or − and if its left-hand context is an operator other than ⟨multiplying operator⟩. Since the first condition does not hold, there is no handle here.

| (d) | 6, 3, 9 | ⟨adding operator⟩
 ⟨term⟩
 (
 ⊢ | A) × A⊣ |

In the next steps, A is a handle and so is the resulting variable ⟨primary⟩.

| (e) | 6, 3, 9, 6, 3 | ⟨term⟩
 ⟨adding operator⟩
 ⟨term⟩
 (
 ⊢ |) × A⊣ |

Now the condition mentioned in step (c) for ⟨term⟩ being a handle holds, after which the top three symbols in the stack constitute a handle.

(f)   6, 3, 9, 6, 3, 1, 2   ⟨*arithmetic expression*⟩   ) × A⊣
                                                        (
                                                        ⊢

After putting the) in the top of the stack, there is another handle
on top of *Holdstack*.

(g)   6, 3, 9, 6, 3, 1, 2, 5   ⟨*primary*⟩   × A⊣
                                                        ⊢

The variable ⟨*primary*⟩ is not a handle this time.

(h)   6, 3, 9, 6, 3, 1, 2, 5, 7   ⟨*multiplying operator*⟩   A⊣
                                                        ⟨*primary*⟩
                                                        ⊢

Again, A and the resulting ⟨*primary*⟩ are handles.

(i)   6, 3, 9, 6, 3, 1, 2, 5,   ⟨*term*⟩   ⊣
                7, 6, 3   ⟨*multiplying operator*⟩
                                                        ⟨*primary*⟩
                                                        ⊢

(j)   6, 3, 9, 6, 3, 1, 2, 5   ⟨*term*⟩   ⊣
                7, 6, 3, 4   ⊢

(k)   6, 3, 9, 6, 3, 1, 2, 5,   ⟨*arithmetic expression*⟩   ⊣
                7, 6, 3, 4, 5   ⊢

And the process is done, having reduced the input to the string
⊢ ⟨*arithmetic expression*⟩ ⊣.

10.5   *bounded contexts*

Right-bounded-context grammars set contextual requirements for
uniquely identifying the handle, the leftmost prime phrase, in a sentential form.   Now let us look at a further generalization of this class
of grammars.

Definition 10.3:   Let $\alpha \rightarrow x_1 x_2 \cdots x_n$ be a production in the production set of a grammar G.   Then let $\bar{s}$ be a sentential form expressed
as follows:

$$\bar{s} = \bar{a}b_1b_2 \cdots b_jx_1x_2 \cdots x_nc_1c_2 \cdots c_k\bar{d}$$

The production is *bounded context* $(j, k)[BC(j, k)]$ if and only if $x_1x_2 \cdots x_n$, being a prime phrase in $\bar{s}$, implies that it is a prime phrase in any sentential form of the following composition.

$$\bar{s}' = \bar{a}'b_1b_2 \cdots b_jx_1x_2 \cdots x_nc_1c_2 \cdots c_k\bar{d}'$$

Definition 10.4:   Suppose each production in a grammar G is $BC(j_i, k_i)$. Then and only then, the grammar is $BC(j', k')$, where

$$j' = \max_i j_i \quad \text{and} \quad k' = \max_i k_i$$

This definition states formally a restriction on grammars very similar to the RBC definitions (Definitions 10.1 and 10.2). The only difference is that, in the bounded-context case, the contextual test applies to all prime phrases, not just the handle.

The bounded-context restriction is a more severe test than the right-bounded-context one. First, clearly all bounded-context grammars are right bounded context, since the handle is a prime phrase. On the other hand, there are right-bounded-context grammars in which other prime phrases do not always satisfy the context restrictions. Below is an example of a grammar that is right bounded context but not bounded context. The example comes from Knuth.

$$G = (\{A, B, C, D\}, \{\sigma, \alpha, \beta\}, \Pi, \sigma)$$

where

$$\Pi = \{\sigma \to A\alpha D \quad :1$$
$$\sigma \to B\alpha\beta \quad :2$$
$$\alpha \to C\alpha \quad :3$$
$$\alpha \to C \quad :4$$
$$\beta \to D \quad :5\}$$

It is not hard to show that the language produced by G is as follows:

$$\Lambda(G) = \{AC^mD, BC^mD \mid m \geq 1\}$$

Now, in the sentence

$$AC^{m-1}CD$$

the right-hand C is the handle, corresponding to production 4. After that, there is a succession of forms $AC^k\alpha D$, in which the phrase $C\alpha$ is a handle, corresponding to production 3. Finally, we arrive at

$$A\alpha D$$

which is itself a handle.

A similar argument for the sentence

$$BC^{m-1}CD$$

will illustrate that the grammar is, in fact, RBC(2, 1). However, it is not BC(j, k) for *any* j and k! The trouble comes with the potential prime phrase at the end of the sentence, the symbol D. A right context restriction assumes that all possible reductions to the left have been taken care of before D is even considered, so there is always a form similar to AαD. We need only look two symbols to the left. If they are Aα, D is not a handle. If they are Bα, then D is, indeed, a handle. However, in the bounded-context case, the issue must be decidable at any time, for any prime phrase. Since the key symbol is on the far left, and the candidate phrase D is on the far right, we have to look n + 1 symbols to the left to find out whether D is a prime phrase. But n + 1 can be arbitrarily large, depending on the sentence size, and so no promise can be made for a limit on the left context size.

This example of a grammar that is right-bounded-context but not bounded-context shows that the set of bounded-context grammars is a *proper subset* of the set of right-bounded-context grammars.

problems

1.   (*a*) Show that if a production is RBC(j, k), it is RBC(j′, k′) for all j′ ≥ j and k′ ≥ k.

   (*b*) Show that Definition 10.2 defines a j′ and k′ such that every production is RBC(j′, k′).

2.   Show that production 1 in the example grammar in Section 10.4 is RBC(1, 1).

3.   Work through the algorithm as in Section 10.4 with the following strings:

   (*a*) A + A + A

   (*b*) A $\times$ (A + A)

4.   For the following production sets, tell whether each production is RBC(j, k), BC(j, k), or neither, and give a value for j and k if they exist.

   (*a*) $\Pi = \{\sigma \rightarrow A\beta\gamma$:1
   $\alpha \rightarrow \alpha A$:2
   $\alpha \rightarrow A$:3
   $\gamma \rightarrow A\gamma$:4
   $\gamma \rightarrow A$:5
   $\beta \rightarrow A$:6$\}$

(b) $\Pi = \{\sigma \to \alpha\beta$:1
$\phantom{\Pi = \{}\alpha \to \alpha A$:2
$\phantom{\Pi = \{}\beta \to A$:3
$\phantom{\Pi = \{}\beta \to B\beta$:4
$\phantom{\Pi = \{}\beta \to B$:5}

(c) $\Pi = \{\sigma \to B\alpha$:1
$\phantom{\Pi = \{}\sigma \to A\beta$:2
$\phantom{\Pi = \{}\alpha \to C\alpha$:3
$\phantom{\Pi = \{}\alpha \to C$:4
$\phantom{\Pi = \{}\beta \to C\beta$:5
$\phantom{\Pi = \{}\beta \to C$:6}

5. Are the grammars defined above RBC(j, k), BC(j, k), or neither? Give values for j and k if they exist.

6. Write a program to translate sentences generated by an RBC(j, k) grammar. The contexts j and k are arbitrary, but can be assumed to have a reasonable bound.

11

precedence grammars

The bounded-context algorithms described in Chapter 10 provide us with a means of translating sentences without backtracking. They allow a bottom-up parsing routine to find out for sure whether a possible handle of the string is, in fact, a handle. But the translator is still not performing at its maximum possible efficiency. It must search for handles and then compare them to see if the contexts match. But we might ask for still another improvement. Is it possible to construct a nontrivial grammar such that the handle stands out so that an extensive search is avoided? If so, the step for comparing and searching for the handle would be shortened.

To see why this possibility might exist, let us reexamine the procedure for translating arithmetic expressions developed in Chapter 2, which uses push-down stacks and precedence rules for the operators. Although an arithmetic expression is constructed of phrases, some of them deeply nested and structured, there is no need for a complex search algorithm to find the prime phrases. In the case of arithmetic expressions, the nested phrases are always denoted either explicitly by parentheses or implicitly by the precedence rules applied to the arithmetic operators. The operands of the operators are passed directly along with no processing necessary.

Thus, for example, a stack translation of the expression analyzed in Chapter 10 would be as follows. The starting configuration is

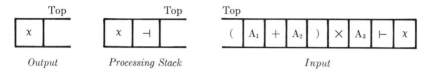

Store the left parenthesis (considered an operator) on the *Processing Stack* and pass the operand directly through to *Outlist,* resulting in

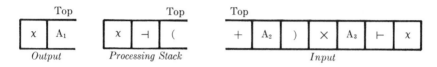

Since + has a higher priority than (, the next two steps result in

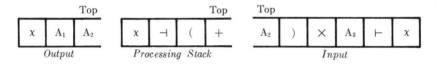

But) has a lower priority than +, so we get

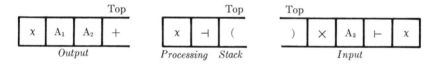

The symbols (and) cancel, according to the algorithm, with no entry placed in *Outlist.* The × operator has a higher priority than ⊣, and so the result of the next two steps is

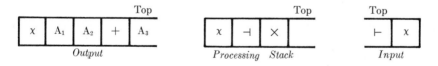

Since × has a higher priority than ⊢, the final output string is

$$A_1 A_2 + A_1 \times$$

In a sense, the phrase structure of the arithmetic expression has been determined by examining the comparative precedence of a leading operator in the input string over the top operator in the operator stack. Although there is a context check in the sense that the algorithm does examine a symbol ahead in the input string, there is no extensive search for phrases within the stack as was necessary in the bounded-context parser.

It is possible to develop an analogous concept for defining a subset of context-free grammars. This subset, in turn, has similarly nice translation properties. It was introduced in 1966 by N. Wirth [9] in conjunction with his definition of an ALGOL-like language called EULER. An earlier form of this type of language was produced by R. W. Floyd [12] but his translator had to deal with ambiguity and thus required backtracking.

11.1   *precedence relations*

The restricted grammars introduced previously imposed a requirement on the behavior of sentential forms during the translation process. The restriction below will involve relations between symbols appearing adjacent in a sentential form, where these relations are derived from the productions themselves. Thus the restrictions are placed on the productions rather than on strings produced by them. The relations will allow the translator to *parenthesize* the string and thus identify the handle.

The first relation, designated $\doteq$, is between symbols that are adjacent *within* a prime phrase. For example, let x_1 and x_2 be symbols, variable or terminal. The relation

$$x_1 \doteq x_2$$

holds if and only if there is a production

$$\xi \rightarrow \bar{y} x_1 x_2 \bar{z}$$

in the production set of the grammar. The substrings $\bar{y}$ and $\bar{z}$ can be null. Note that the definition is not symmetric in x_1 and x_2. That is, given $x_1 \doteq x_2$, there is no reason to conclude that $x_2 \doteq x_1$, which may or may not be the case depending on the particular grammar. The notation $\doteq$, while usefully suggestive in some ways, can be misleading since it has none of the properties of an equivalence relation.

The next two relations are more complex. Recall the concept introduced earlier of the left terminal set and the right terminal set of a variable. Respectively, they were the sets of extreme left- and right-hand terminal symbols of all sentential forms produced by the variable. Generalizing to sets of all symbols, terminal and variable, we can define left-hand sets and right-hand sets. These sets are designated $LHS(\alpha)$ and $RHS(\alpha)$, respectively, where α is the root variable. Two symbols, x_1 and x_2, are related in the form

$$x_1 <\cdot\ x_2$$

if and only if they can occur adjacent in a sentential form in which x_2 is the start of a phrase and no complete phrase is to the left of x_2. The relation holds if there is a production

$$\alpha \to \bar{y}x_1\beta\bar{z}$$

where x_2 is in $LHS(\beta)$, that is, where x_2 is a symbol on the left-hand side of some string produced by β. As with the $\doteq$ relation, do not be fooled by the $<\cdot$ relation. It has, in general, none of the properties of a normal order relation. No conclusions can be drawn from the statement $x_1 <\cdot\ x_2$ about the precedence relations between any other pair of symbols, or about other relations between x_1 and x_2.

The final relation, $\cdot>$, is defined similarly to $<\cdot$, with one additional twist. Again let x_1 and x_2 be two symbols in a grammar. They are related in the form

$$x_1 \cdot> x_2$$

if x_1 can terminate a phrase in the context of x_2 to the right. That is, the form holds if there is a production

$$\alpha \to \bar{y}\xi x_2\bar{z}$$

where x_1 is in the $RHS(\xi)$, or it holds if there is a production

$$\alpha \to \bar{y}\xi\beta\bar{z}$$

where x_1 is in $RHS(\xi)$ and x_2 is in $LHS(\beta)$.

11.2   *generating precedence relations—example*

To find the precedence relation among the symbols of a grammar, it is necessary to generate the left and right sets for all of the variables in the language. In Section 9.2, a simple algorithm for doing this task was presented for sets of terminal symbols, and it can be easily extended to the general case of both terminal and variable symbols. It will be assumed that job has been done, so that the right- and left-hand

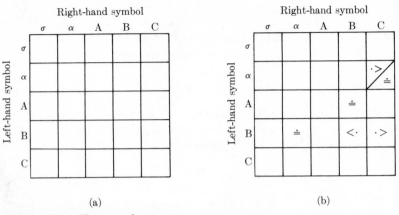

(a)   (b)

Figure 11.1   The precedence
table for G_1

sets are stored in memory and can be accessed during the generation
routines.

Let us look first at a simple example grammar and determine
its precedence relations.   Then the procedure can be generalized.   Let

$$G_1 = (\{\sigma, \alpha\}, \{A, B, C\}, \Pi, \sigma)$$

where

$$\Pi = \{\sigma \rightarrow AB\alpha C \qquad :1$$
$$\alpha \rightarrow B\alpha \qquad :2$$
$$\alpha \rightarrow B \qquad :3\}$$

The relations between symbols can be conveniently expressed in the
form of a table, called a *precedence table*.   The empty precedence
table for G_1 is shown in Figure 11.1(a).

The reader can verify that the left- and right-hand sets are

$$LHS(\sigma) = \{A\}$$
$$LHS(\alpha) = \{B\}$$
$$RHS(\sigma) = \{C\}$$
$$RHS(\alpha) = \{\alpha, B\}$$

Now the table can be filled by applying the three definitions to each
of the productions, one at a time.   Take production 1, for example.
By definition of the $\doteq$ relation, it can be seen that

$$A \doteq B$$
$$B \doteq \alpha$$

and

$$\alpha \doteq C$$

Further, applying the definition of the $<\cdot$ relation gives

$$B <\cdot LHS(\alpha)$$

or, in other words, that

$$B <\cdot B$$

Finally, by applying the definition of $\cdot>$,

$$RHS(\alpha) \cdot> C$$
or
$$\alpha \cdot> C$$
$$B \cdot> C$$

The other two productions do not add any relations to the table.   The precedence table, filled in, appears in Figure 11.1(b).

The example above illustrates two additional facts about precedence relations that you should note.

1.   Not all pairs of symbols exhibit precedence relations [for example, the pair (A, C) in the table above].
2.   Some pairs of symbols may have more than one precedence relation [for example, (α, C) in the table above].

11.3   generating precedence relations—algorithm

The example above suggests a general approach to finding the precedence table for a grammar.   All definitions for the relations derive from adjacent symbols in the argument of a production.   To generate the precedence relations then, we need only step from production to production, generating relations from each pair of adjacent symbols in its argument.   To simplify the exposition, the algorithm presented here will treat just one production argument.

Before getting to the algorithm, let us establish some simple functions and subroutines, and define our variables.

Argument(I) is the production argument being treated.   It is a string of symbols.   Assume, also, that the left-hand and right-hand sets of a variable X have been generated and stored in $LHS(X)$ and $RHS(X)$, respectively.

The most complex subroutine needed is called *Fill* (X, Y, Z) and is charged with filling the precedence table with the proper symbols. The arguments X and Z are symbols from *Argument*(I). Y is one of the relations, $\doteq$, $<\cdot$, or $\cdot>$.   The action of *Fill* varies according to the relation Y, as follows.

If Y is $\doteq$ *Fill* sets $X \doteq Z$.
If Y is $<\cdot$ *Fill* sets $X <\cdot$ a for all a $\in RHS(Z)$
If Y is $\cdot>$ *Fill* sets $X \cdot>$ a for all a $\in LHS(Z)$ and sets a $\cdot>$ b for all
    a $\in RHS(X)$, b $\in LHS(Z)$ (if X is a variable)

A final function, $Terminal(X)$ is a predicate, a Boolean test with value **True** or **False,** depending on whether X is a terminal symbol or a variable.

The procedure is simple and straightforward. There are two symmetrical parts to the algorithm. Control is in one or the other of them depending on whether the previous symbol read was a terminal or variable symbol. The flow chart for the algorithm is shown in Figure 11.2.

11.4   precedence grammars

Now it is time to put together the previous discussions and define another form of restricted grammar.

Definition 11.1: A grammar, G = (Σ, T, Π, σ), is a *precedence grammar* if and only if every pair of symbols in $\Sigma \cup T$ has at most one precedence relation, and no two arguments of productions in Π are identical.

In Problem 1 you will be asked to show that, if s_1 and s_2 appear adjacent in a sentential form, at least one precedence relation holds between them. Putting this fact together with Definition 11.1, we can see that exactly one precedence relation holds between every pair of adjacent symbols in a sentential form of a precedence grammar. This pseudo-parenthesizing is the property that allows the simple translation of sentences generated by this kind of grammar.

Let us test and see if the simple grammar below for arithmetic expressions is a precedence grammar.

$$G_2 = (\{A, +, \times,)\, (\}, \{\langle sentence\rangle, \langle arithmetic\ expression\rangle,$$
$$\langle term\rangle, \langle primary\rangle\}, \Pi, \langle sentence\rangle)$$

$\Pi = \{\langle sentence\rangle \rightarrow \langle arithmetic\ expression\rangle$:1
$\langle arithmetic\ expression\rangle \rightarrow \langle arithmetic\ expression\rangle$
     $+ \langle term\rangle$:2
$\langle arithmetic\ expression\rangle \rightarrow \langle term\rangle$:3
$\langle term\rangle \rightarrow \langle term\rangle \times \langle primary\rangle$:4
$\langle term\rangle \rightarrow \langle primary\rangle$:5
$\langle primary\rangle \rightarrow A$:6
$\langle primary\rangle \rightarrow (\langle arithmetic\ expression\rangle)$:7$\}$

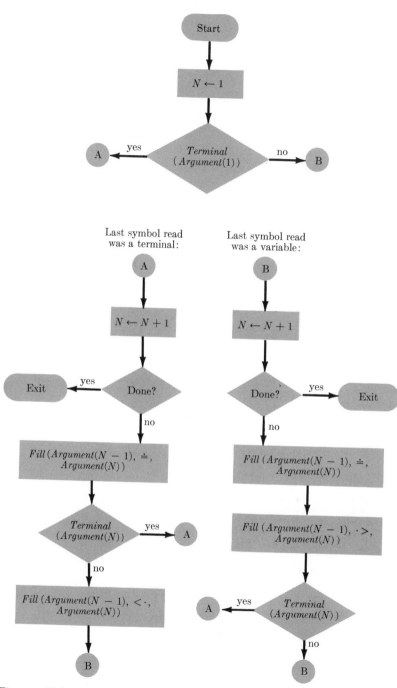

Figure 11.2 An algorithm for generating precedence relations from a single production

	⟨sentence⟩	⟨arithmetic expression⟩	⟨term⟩	⟨primary⟩	A	(	)	+	×
⟨sentence⟩									
⟨arithmetic expression⟩							≐	≐	
⟨term⟩							·>	·>	≐
⟨primary⟩							·>	·>	·>
A							·>	·>	·>
(		≐/<·	<·	<·	<·	<·			
)							>	·>	·>
+			≐/<·	<·	<·	<·			
×				≐	<·	<·			

$RHS(\langle sentence \rangle) = \{\langle arithmetic\ expression \rangle, \langle term \rangle, \langle primary \rangle,), A\}$

$LHS(\langle sentence \rangle) = \{\langle arithmetic\ expression \rangle, \langle term \rangle, \langle primary \rangle, (, A\}$

$RHS(\langle arithmetic\ expression \rangle) = \{\langle term \rangle, \langle primary \rangle,), A\}$

$LHS(\langle arithmetic\ expression \rangle) = \{\langle arithmetic\ expression \rangle, \langle term \rangle, \langle primary \rangle, (, A\}$

$RHS(\langle term \rangle) = \{\langle primary \rangle,), A\}$

$LHS(\langle term \rangle) = \{\langle term \rangle, \langle primary \rangle, (, A\}$

$RHS(\langle primary \rangle) = \{), A\}$

$LHS(\langle primary \rangle) = \{(, A\}$

Figure 11.3 Right-hand sets, left-hand sets, and precedence table for grammar G_2

The precedence table for G_2 is shown in Figure 11.3 and G_2 is not a precedence grammar. As will often turn out to be the case, however, a precedence grammar can be constructed from G_2. For example, the following grammar, G_2', is a precedence grammar for the same language as that generated by G_2. Clearly, no damage has been done to the overall structure of the translation tree.

$$G_2' = (\{A, +, \times, (,)\}, \{\langle sentence \rangle, \langle arithmetic\ expression \rangle',$$
$$\langle arithmetic\ expression \rangle, \langle term \rangle, \langle term \rangle', \langle primary \rangle\}, \Pi,$$
$$\langle sentence \rangle)$$

$$\Pi = \{\langle sentence \rangle \rightarrow \langle arithmetic\ expression \rangle' \qquad :1$$

$\langle arithmetic\ expression \rangle \rightarrow \langle arithmetic\ expression \rangle$	:2
$\langle arithmetic\ expression \rangle \rightarrow \langle arithmetic\ expression \rangle$	
$\quad + \langle term \rangle'$	:3
$\langle arithmetic\ expression \rangle \rightarrow \langle term \rangle$	:4
$\langle term \rangle' \rightarrow \langle term \rangle$	:5
$\langle term \rangle \rightarrow \langle term \rangle \times \langle primary \rangle$	:6
$\langle term \rangle \rightarrow \langle primary \rangle$	:7
$\langle primary \rangle \rightarrow A$	:8
$\langle primary \rangle \rightarrow (\langle arithmetic\ expression \rangle)$	:9\}

11.5   translation algorithm

Assume that we have a precedence grammar G and a sentence written in it, which we wish to translate. The first step, of course, is to build the proper tables for use by the translator. Figure 11.4 illustrates the complete flow of the translation process. Notice that, even if several sentences in the same grammars are to be translated, the construction of the tables only needs to be done once. Given the precedence tables as already constructed, let us proceed to translation itself.

We have mentioned that every pair of adjacent symbols in a legal sentential form generated by a precedence grammar exhibits one and only one precedence relation. Thus, given a sentence, it is possible to imagine a relation between each neighboring pair of symbols, as illustrated below. Let

$$s_1 s_2 s_3 s_4 s_5 s_6$$

be a sentential form and then let

$$s_1 <\cdot\ s_2 \doteq s_3 <\cdot\ s_4 \cdot> s_5 \doteq s_6$$

be the same sentence with precedence relations inserted between the appropriate symbols.

Some reflection and reference back to the definitions should show that the precedence relations have pseudo-parenthesized the string. For example, in the string above, s_2 starts a phrase subordinate to the one containing s_1, while the symbol s_3 is at the same phrase level as s_2. By merely examining the string, then, we can see that the

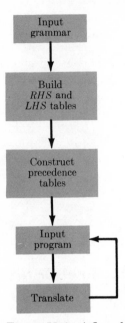

Figure 11.4   A flow chart for
the translation process

handle is s_4. If we substitute for s_4 the root α of the production
of which it is the argument, the result is

$$s_1 \lessdot s_2 \doteq s_3 \alpha s_5 \doteq s_6$$

and the missing precedence relations are filled in, say, as follows:

$$s_1 \lessdot s_2 \doteq s_3 \gtrdot \alpha \gtrdot s_5 \doteq s_6$$

The relations are new because s_4 is gone and α is a new symbol in the.
string.   Now the substring $s_2 s_3$ appears to be the prime phrase.   Let β
be its root, resulting in

$$s_1 \beta \alpha \gtrdot s_5 \doteq s_6$$

The missing precedence relations are again filled in.

This discussion suggests a simple algorithm for translating sentences in a precedence grammar by using the precedence table.   The
algorithm is similar to that discussed for arithmetic expression in
Section 11.1.

Notice that the handle is delimited on the right by the first
occurrence of the $\gtrdot$ relation when scanning the string from left
to right.   Note also that since the productions of a precedence gram-

mar have unique arguments, there is no ambiguity in deciding which substitution is to be made. The algorithm is deterministic, with one output parse (if the sentence is legal). Thus a precedence grammar, having unique production arguments, generates an unambiguous language, a nice bonus!

As usual, the symbols will be held in *Holdstack* as they are read off the input list. The function $Prec(X, Y)$ returns one of three values depending on whether the precedence relation between symbol X and symbol Y is $<\cdot$, $\doteq$, or $\cdot>$. The function $Root(Argument)$ is the root of the production that has *Argument* as its right-hand side, and $Index(Argument)$ is that production's index. *Outlist* is, once again, the historical trace file containing the output of the parser.

A special symbol, *Marker*, designates a $<\cdot$ relation and is stored on *Holdstack* at appropriate points. The other special symbols, $\vdash$ and $\dashv$, designate, respectively, the left and right terminators of the input string. The sentence root σ appears only once, as the root of a production of the form

$$\sigma \rightarrow \vdash \alpha \dashv$$

Initially, *Holdstack* contains a *Marker* followed by a $\vdash$, and the input string is terminated by two $\dashv$'s. The entry

$$\dashv \cdot > \dashv$$

has also been made in the precedence table. These assumptions allow the algorithm to recognize the completion of the translation as the existence of a σ on top of *Holdstack*. Figure 11.5 shows the flow chart for the translation algorithm.

To see how the termination of the algorithm works, suppose the translation is nearly done, at the following stage.

Holdstack   *Inlist*

Let us step through the procedure from this point. We know from the production and the definitions that $\vdash \doteq \alpha$. Therefore α is pushed on *Holdstack*. Now $\alpha \doteq \dashv$ for the same reason, and now we have the following.

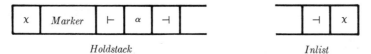

Holdstack   *Inlist*

Now $\dashv \cdot > \dashv$, so *Holdstack* is popped until *Marker*. *Argument* is $\vdash \alpha \dashv$, and $Root(Argument)$, then, is σ.

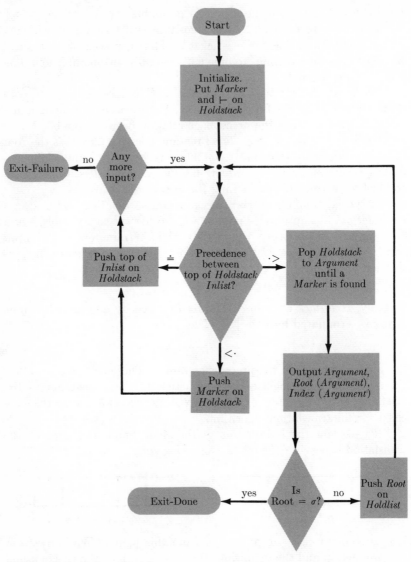

Figure 11.5   A flow chart for
the precedence translation

11.6   *precedence functions*

The precedence table can take up substantial space in memory, even
for simple precedence grammars. Not only that, it is only sparsely
filled with meaningful entries. Storing it in memory as a two-dimensional table takes up space and uses it very inefficiently. Is there
some way of compressing it?

Of course, there are several general techniques for compressing sparse tables in memory, but these methods usually require more time both in searching for values and in construction. Since the table is only built once, efficiency in construction time is not too important, but since the algorithm refers to it constantly, searching efficiency is very important. One solution to this problem is through the use of *precedence functions*. These functions apply numerical values to the symbols of the grammar in such a way as to allow the precedence relations to be easily determined.

Definition 11.2:   Two functions, f and g, are called precedence functions of a precedence grammar if they have the following properties for every pair of symbols (s_1, s_2) in the grammar.

(a)   If $s_1 \doteq s_2$, then $f(s_1) = g(s_2)$.   (Remember, f and g apply numerical values to s_1 and s_2.)

(b)   If $s_1 <\cdot s_2$, then $f(s_1) < g(s_2)$.

(c)   If $s_1 \cdot> s_2$, then $f(s_1) > g(s_2)$.

Two points need to be made right away about precedence functions. First, they are not unique. If one set of precedence functions exists for a grammar, then an infinite number of precedence functions exist for it. As just one example of how to generate an infinite number of them, add any constant number c to all values of f and g. Clearly, the precedence relationships still hold. Similarly, multiply them by a constant, or raise them to a power, and they are still in the same relationship. The second point is that it is not always true that a precedence function exists for a precedence grammar. Take the following grammar, for example:

$$G = (\{\sigma, \alpha, \beta, \delta\}, \{A, B, C\}, \Pi, \sigma)$$

where

$$\begin{aligned}
\Pi = \{\sigma &\to \alpha &&:1 \\
\sigma &\to \delta &&:2 \\
\alpha &\to AB &&:3 \\
\alpha &\to A\beta &&:4 \\
\alpha &\to \alpha B &&:5 \\
\delta &\to \delta\beta &&:6 \\
\delta &\to \alpha &&:7 \\
\beta &\to C &&:8\}
\end{aligned}$$

Figure 11.6 shows the precedence table for G.

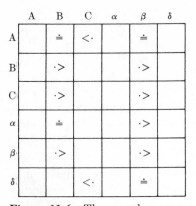

	A	B	C	α	β	δ
A		≐	<·		≐	
B		·>			·>	
C		·>			·>	
α		≐			·>	
β		·>			·>	
δ			<·		≐	

Figure 11.6   The precedence table for G

Assume that there is a set of precedence functions f and g for G. Then, from the table and the definitions, we get

$$f(A) = g(B)$$
$$f(\alpha) = g(B)$$
$$f(\alpha) > g(\beta)$$
$$f(A) = g(\beta)$$

which implies

$$f(A) = g(B) = f(\alpha) > g(\beta) = f(A)$$
or $$f(A) > f(A)$$

which is impossible.   Thus no precedence function can exist for G.

There are several methods for producing precedence functions, if they exist, from precedence grammars.   One of the simplest algorithms, iterative in nature, is described by Floyd [12] in his research paper on a similar (but not equivalent) class of grammars.   The three steps of the algorithms are as follows:

Algorithm: **PF**

PF 1:   (Initialize.) $f(s_i) \leftarrow g(s_i) \leftarrow 1$ for all i;
PF 2:   (Loop iteration.)   **For** all pairs of indices (i, j) **Do**
      If $s_i \cdot > s_j$ **And** $f(s_i) \leq g(s_j)$ **Then** $f(s_i) \leftarrow g(s_j) + 1$;
      If $s_i \doteq s_j$ **And** $f(s_i) \neq g(s_j)$ **Then** make the smaller of the two equal to the larger;
      If $s_i <\cdot s_j$ **And** $f(s_i) \geq g(s_j)$ **Then** $g(s_j) \leftarrow f(s_i) + 1$;

PF 3: (Repeat rule.)   Repeat *PF 2* either until the process converges, that is, until no modifications on f or g are performed in a pass through *PF 2*, or until any f or g value is greater than 2N where N is the number of symbols in $T \cup \Sigma$, $(N = \#(T \cup \Sigma))$.

Careful observation of the algorithm will show that, if it can make a pass through *PF 2* without having to make an alteration in f or g, the two functions must be precedence functions for the grammar. Furthermore, it can be shown rather easily that if there are precedence functions for the grammar, the maximum of f and g generated by this algorithm must be equal to or less than twice the total number of symbols in the grammar. Thus, if the algorithm produces a value of f or g greater than 2N, it has failed to produce the precedence functions, and none exist.

problems

1. Given a grammar
    $$G = (\Sigma, T, \Pi, \sigma)$$
    Show that, if x_1 and x_2 are two symbols in $\Sigma \cup T$ and if $\bar{y}x_1x_2\bar{z}$ is a sentential form for G, then at least one of the three relations $<\cdot$, $\cdot>$, or $\doteq$ must hold between x_1 and x_2.

2. Step through the development of the right- and left-hand sets and precedence table in Figure 11.3.

3. (a) Derive the right- and left-hand sets for the grammar G_2 in Section 11.4. (b) Develop the precedence table for G_2' in the same section. And (c) explain the difference between G_2 and G_2'.

4. What do the empty spaces in the precedence table signify about the language generated by a precedence grammar?

5. (a) Modify G_2' of Section 11.4 to the form required for application of the translating algorithm for precedence grammars and (b) generate its precedence table.

6. Parenthesize with precedence relations the following sentential forms generated by G_2' above and identify the handle in each case.

    (a) $\vdash$A + A$\dashv$

    (b) $\vdash$(A + A) × A$\dashv$

    (c) $\vdash$(⟨*arithmetic expression*⟩) × A$\dashv$

7. For each of the forms in Problem 6, apply the algorithm to the handle and show the newly transformed string with the new precedence relations.

8. Implement the precedence translation algorithm.

9. Prove that, if a set of precedence functions exists for a precedence grammar, there exists an s_j in the symbol set for which there exists no s_i such that $s_j \cdot > s_i$, and there exists no s_i such that $s_i < \cdot s_j$. That is, s_j is, in some sense, a lower bound of the symbol set. (Hint: Use the number properties of the values of f and g.)

10. Show that, if f and g are precedence functions generated by PF, there exists an s_i such that either $f(s_i) = 1$ or $g(s_i) = 1$.

11. Prove that, if f and g are precedence functions generated by the PF algorithm, then for every s_i either (a) $f(s_i) = 1$; (b) there is an s_j such that $f(s_i) = g(s_j)$; or (c) there is an s_j such that $f(s_i) = g(s_j) + 1$.

12. Show that the results from Problems 10 and 11 imply that a pair of precedence functions generated by PF cannot have a value of f or g exceeding 2N where N is the total number of symbols in the grammar.

13. (a) Show that, if algorithm PF generates a value of f or g greater than 2N, there exists a set of symbols for which the precedence relations "cycle." That is, there exists a string

    $$s_1, s_2, s_3, \ldots, s_{2n}$$

    for which

    $$s_1 \leq \cdot s_2$$
    $$s_3 \cdot \geq s_2$$
    $$\cdot$$
    $$\cdot$$
    $$\cdot$$
    $$s_1 \cdot \geq s_{2n}$$

    (b) Show that, if such a cycle exists, no precedence functions can exist. Thus, if algorithm PF gets hung up on such a cycle, no precedence functions exist for the grammar.

14. Apply the PF algorithm to the precedence grammar G_2' defined in Section 11.4.

bibliography

This bibliography is not intended to be complete. It contains a somewhat personal selection of articles deemed to be of interest in pursuing topics discussed in this book further. A good, exhaustive bibliography can be found in the survey by J. Feldman and D. Gries [2]. The references are divided into a few topical groupings for convenience.

Surveys: There have been some good general surveys published. Among the most interesting are the following:

[1]   Davis, R. M.: "Programming Language Processors," *Advances in Computers,* vol. 7, pp. 117–180.
[2]   Feldman, J., and D. Gries: "Translator Writing Systems," *Communications of the Association for Computing Machinery,* vol. 11, pp. 77–113, February 1966.

Theory of Context-Free Grammars: N. Chomsky's books are basic source material. The other two are good texts on the topic.

[3]   Chomsky, N.: *Syntactic Structures,* Mouton, The Hague, 1957.
[4]   Chomsky, N.: *Aspects of the Theory of Syntax,* M.I.T., Cambridge, Mass., 1965.
[5]   Ginsburg, S.: *The Mathematical Theory of Context-Free Languages,* McGraw-Hill, New York, 1966.

[6]   Hopcroft, J. E., and J. D. Ullman: *Formal Languages and Their Relation to Automata*, Addison-Wesley, Reading, Mass., 1967.

Computer Language Definition: Many attempts have been made to define the syntax of computer languages formally.   Here are a few examples.

[7]   Naur, P. (ed): "Report on the Algorithmic Language ALGOL 60," *Communications of the Association for Computing Machinery*, vol. 3, pp. 299–314, May 1960.

[8]   Steel, T. B. (ed): *Formal Language Description Languages for Computer Programming*, North-Holland Publishing Company, Amsterdam, 1971.

[9]   Wirth, N.: *A Programming Language for the 360 Computer*, Stanford University Computer Science Department Technical Report C553, December 1966.

Parsing: This is only a small selection of the numerous papers published on the topic.   They cover areas discussed in the book.

[10]   Cheatham, T. E., and K. Sattley: "Syntax Directed Compiling," *Proceedings Spring Joint Computer Conference*, pp. 31–57, 1964.

[11]   Earley, J.: "An Efficient Context-Free Parsing Algorithm," *Communications of the Association for Computing Machinery*, vol. 13, pp. 94–102, February 1970.

[12]   Floyd, R. W.: "Bounded Context Syntactic Analysis," *Communications of the Association for Computing Machinery*, vol. 7, pp. 62–67, February 1964.

[13]   Floyd, R. W.: "Syntactic Analysis and Operator Precedence," *Journal of the Association for Computing Machinery*, vol. 10, pp. 316–333, July 1963.

[14]   Graham, R. M.: "Bounded Context Translation," *Proceedings Spring Joint Computer Conference*, pp. 17–29, 1964.

[15]   Irons, E. T.: "Structural Connections in Formal Languages," *Communications of the Association for Computing Machinery*, vol. 7, pp. 67–72, February 1964.

[16]   Knuth, D. E.: "On the Translation of Languages from Left to Right," *Information and Control*, vol. 8, pp. 607–639, October 1965.

[17]   Korenjak, A. J.: "A Practical Method for Constructing LR(k) Processors," *Communications of the Association for Computing Machinery*, vol. 12, pp. 613–623, November 1969.

[18]   Ross, D. T.: "On Context and Ambiguity in Parsing," *Communications of the Association for Computing Machinery*, vol. 7, pp. 131–133, February 1964.

[19] Wirth, N., and H. Weber: "EULER—A Generalization of ALGOL, and Its Formal Definition: Part I; Part II," *Communications of the Association for Computing Machinery,* vol. 9, pp. 13–25, 89–99, January and February 1966.

Compiler Writing: These references show how and where the parsing process fits into the writing of a compiler.

[20] Grau, A. A., V. Hill, and H. Langmaack: *Translation of ALGOL 60,* Springer-Verlag, Berlin, 1967.
[21] Lee, J. A. N.: *The Anatomy of a Compiler,* Reinhold, New York, 1967.
[22] McKeeman, W. M., J. J. Horning, and D. B. Wortman: *A Compiler Generator,* Prentice-Hall, Englewood Cliffs, N.J., 1970.
[23] Randell, B., and L. J. Russell: *ALGOL 60 Implementation,* Academic, New York, 1964.

Natural-Language Translation: An important area of work that draws on language and parsing theory is natural-language processing. The following are good introductions to the subject.

[24] Borko, H. (ed): *Automated Language Processing,* Wiley, New York, 1967.
[25] Friedman, J.: *A Computer Model of Transformational Grammar,* American Elsevier, New York, 1971.
[26] Garvin, P. L. (ed): *Natural Language and the Computer,* McGraw-Hill, New York, 1963.
[27] Hays, D. G.: *Introduction to Computational Linguistics,* American Elsevier, New York, 1967.
[28] Sager, Naomi: "Syntactic Analysis and Natural Language," *Advances in Computers,* vol. 8, pp. 153–187, 1967.

Meta Compilers: The following are a couple of examples of *compiler-compilers,* systems written to accept a formal definition of a language and, using that definition, to compile a program written in that language. The Ingerman book is a very thorough discussion of a particular system.

[29] Ingerman, P. F.: *A Syntax-Oriented Translator,* Academic, New York, 1966.
[30] McClure, R. M.: "TMG—A Syntax Directed Compiler," *Proceedings of the Twentieth Conference of the Association for Computing Machinery,* pp. 262–274, 1965.

index